N. Glenister
30p.

KING ALFRED'S COLLEGE
WINCHESTER

———

To be returned on or before the day marked below :—

PLEASE ENTER ON ISSUE SLIP:

AUTHOR MILLWARD

TITLE The eighteenth centur...

ACCESSION No.

PORTRAITS AND DOCUMENTS

A SERIES OF HISTORICAL SOURCE BOOKS

GENERAL EDITOR: J. S. MILLWARD

The Early Middle Ages edited by **Derek Baker**
871–1216

The Later Middle Ages edited by **Derek Baker**
1216–1485 (in preparation)

The Sixteenth Century edited by **J. S. Millward**
1485–1603

The Seventeenth Century edited by **J. S. Millward**
1603–1714

The Eighteenth Century edited by **J. S. Millward** and
H. P. Arnold-Craft
1714–1783

The Earlier Nineteenth Century edited by **Dennis Holman**
1783–1867

The Later Nineteenth Century edited by **Peter Teed**
(in preparation)

PORTRAITS AND DOCUMENTS

EIGHTEENTH CENTURY

1714–1783

Edited by
J. S. MILLWARD
Senior History Master
Bristol Grammar School

and

H. P. ARNOLD-CRAFT
Senior History Master
Magdalen College School
Oxford

HUTCHINSON EDUCATIONAL

HUTCHINSON EDUCATIONAL LTD

178–202 Great Portland Street, London W1

London Melbourne Sydney
Auckland Bombay Toronto
Johannesburg New York

★

First published 1962
Second impression August 1966

*This book has been set in Fournier, printed in Great Britain
on Smooth Wove paper by Anchor Press and
bound by Wm. Brendon, both of Tiptree, Essex*

Contents

POLITICAL AND CONSTITUTIONAL

RELIGIOUS, ECONOMIC AND SOCIAL

Illustrations

ACKNOWLEDGEMENTS

Acknowledgement is gladly made to the following for permission to use copyright material:

Oxford University Press for some verses from *Poor Fred, The People's Prince* by Sir George Young; Messrs Longmans, Green & Co. Ltd for extracts from *Life of William Pitt, Earl of Chatham* by B. Williams, and *Source Book of Constitutional History from 1660* by D. O. Dykes; Messrs Macmillan & Co. Ltd for extracts from *Correspondence of George III* edited by Sir J. Fortescue; the Essex Record Office and Mr A. C. Edwards for Sir William Shirley's Memorandum printed in his book, *English History from Essex Sources*; the Officer Commanding, The King's Own Yorkshire Light Infantry for part of Lieutenant Montgomery's letter in *History of the King's Own Yorkshire Light Infantry* by H. C. Wylly; His Grace the Earl of Hardwicke for extracts from *Life and Correspondence of the Earl of Hardwicke* by P. Yorke; the Controller of H.M. Stationery Office for material from *The Earl of Egmont's Diary*, the *Calendar of Home Office Papers, George III*— Volume IV, and the *Calendar of State Papers, Colonial*— Volume XXXVII.

The extract from the Royal Archives at Windsor on pages 59–60 is printed by gracious permission of Her Majesty the Queen.

Every effort has been made to trace the owners of copyright material. The editors apologize for any omissions, and would be grateful to know of them, so that acknowledgement may be made in any future editions.

Introduction

The use of a contemporary source-book is probably the easiest way for both teacher and pupil to capture that degree of realism without which the story of man in society must lack conviction. Such books at a relatively low price are difficult to come by, and it was this deficiency which is responsible for the current series, intended for class use by pupils.

The limitations of this type of work are manifold. The subjectivity involved in selection leaves one open to the accusation of unbalance, as indeed does the harsh necessity of restricting the number of documents in any one section. The attempt to cater for the interests and appetites of the Middle School as well as the Sixth Form has encouraged the editors to broaden the range of social and economic documents—possibly at the expense of those concerning political developments in the eighteenth century. Nevertheless it is hoped that, in spite of these inevitable drawbacks, most secondary school children, as well as their teachers, will find here something to interest them, to make them the more curious, and even to make them laugh.

This volume covers the period 1714–83. To avoid duplication, the Industrial Revolution has been left for the next volume on the early nineteenth century, which seems a more appropriate place for it, while the Agricultural Revolution has been included here. As in the earlier volumes in this series, introductory notes have been kept to the minimum, since the editors do not want either to patronize teachers or to prevent pupils asking questions; also, the more notes there are, the less space for documents.

Of the many who have assisted in the production of this collection, Dr J. B. Owen has been an invaluable adviser and an indefatigable scout, giving freely of his time and expert knowledge, and to him the editors are deeply indebted. The publishers have shown great patience with the procrastinations of schoolmasters, while Miss Ann Howgate has guided us dextrously through the pitfalls of publication, earning our further gratitude by her great help with the illustrations.

PORTRAITS

George I

Source: Lord Chesterfield, *Letters (with the Characters)* (1892) iii. p. 1402

Plate 1

George the First was an honest and dull German gentleman, as unfit as unwilling to act the part of a King, which is, to shine and oppress. Lazy and inactive even in his pleasures; which were therefore lowly and sensual. He was coolly intrepid, and indolently benevolent. He was diffident of his own parts, which made him speak little in public and prefer in his social, which were his favourite, hours, the company of wags and buffoons. . . . His views and affections were singly confined to the narrow compass of his electorate. England was too big for him. If he had nothing great as a King, he had nothing bad as a man and if he does not adorn, at least he will not stain the annals of this country. In private life, he would have been loved and esteemed as a good citizen, a good friend, and a good neighbour. Happy were it for Europe, happy for the world, if there were not greater Kings in it!

❖

George II

i.   *Source:* H. Walpole, *Memoirs of the Reign of King George II* (1846) iii. pp. 303–4

Plate 2 (a)

His faults were more the blemishes of a private man than of a King. The affection and tenderness he invariably showed to a people over whom he had unbounded rule [in Hanover] forbid our wondering that he used circumscribed power with moderation [in England]. Often situated in humiliating circumstances, his resentments seldom operated when the power of revenge returned. He bore the ascendant of his Ministers, who seldom were his favourites, with more patience than he suffered any encroachment on his will from his mistresses. Content to bargain for the gratification of his two predominant passions, Hanover and money, he was almost indifferent to the rest of his royal authority, provided exterior observance was not wanting; for he comforted himself if he did not perceive the diminution of Majesty, though it was notorious to all the rest of the world. Yet he was not so totally careless of the affection and interests of his country as his father had been. George the First possessed a sounder understanding and a better temper: yet George the Second gained more by being compared with his eldest son, than he lost if paralleled with his father. . . .

ii. *Source:* Lord Hervey, *Memoirs of the Reign of George II* (1848) i. p. 289

Many ingredients concurred to form this reluctance in his Majesty to bestowing. One was that, taking all his notions from a German measure, he thought every man who served him in England overpaid; another was, that while employments were vacant he saved the salary; but the most prevalent of all was his never having the least inclination to oblige. I do not believe there ever lived a man to whose temper benevolence was so absolutely a stranger. It was a sensation that, I dare say, never accompanied any one act of his power; so that whatever good he did was either extorted from him, or was the adventitious effect of some self-interested act of policy: consequently, if any seeming favour he conferred ever obliged the receiver, it must have been because the man on whom it fell was ignorant of the motives from which the giver bestowed.

❖

Queen Caroline

Source: Lord Hervey, *Memoirs of the Reign of George II* (1848) i. pp. 293–5

Plate 2 (b)

... To most people, however, it was a matter of wonder how the King and Queen could have such persons constantly with them. The truth of the case was, that the King had no taste for better company, and the Queen, though she had a better taste, was forced to mortify her own to please his. Her predominant passion was pride, and the darling pleasure of her soul was power; but she was forced to gratify the one and gain the other, as some people do health, by a strict and painful régime, which few besides herself could have had patience to support, or resolution to adhere to. She was at least seven or eight hours *tête-à-tête* with the King every day, during which time she was generally saying what she did not think, assenting to what she did not believe, and praising what she did not approve; for they were seldom of the same opinion, and he too fond of his own for her ever at first to dare to controvert it; she used to give him her opinion as jugglers do a card, by changing it imperceptibly, and making him believe he held the same with that he first pitched upon. But that which made these *tête-à-têtes* seem heaviest was that he neither liked reading nor being read to (unless it was to sleep): she was forced, like a spider, to spin out of her own bowels all the conversation with which the fly was taken. However, to all this she submitted for the sake of power, and for the reputation of having it; for the vanity of being thought to possess what she desired was equal to the pleasure of the possession itself. But, either for the appearance or the reality, she knew it was absolutely necessary to have interest in her husband, as she was sensible that interest was the measure by which people would always judge of her power. Her every thought, word, and act therefore tended and was calculated to preserve her influence there; to him she sacrificed her time, for him she mortified her inclination; she looked, spake, and breathed but for him, like a weathercock to every capricious blast of his uncertain temper, and governed him (if such influence so gained can bear the name of government) by being as great a slave to him thus ruled, as any other wife could be to a man who ruled her. For all the tedious hours she spent then in watching him whilst he slept, or the heavier task of entertaining him whilst he was awake, her single consolation was in reflecting she had power, and that people in coffee-houses and ruelles[1] were saying she governed this country, without knowing how dear the government of it cost her.

◆

Frederick, Prince of Wales

The Prince of Wales, 'Poor Fred', predeceased his father in 1751.

i. *Source:* Sir G. Young, *Poor Fred, the People's Prince* (1937) p. 223

Here lies poor Fred, who was alive and is dead.
We had rather it had been his Father,
Had it been his brother, better'n any other,
Had it been his sister no one would have missed her,
Had it been the whole generation, all the better for the nation,
But as it's just poor Fred, who was alive and is dead,
There's no more to be said.

ii. *Source:* Lord Hervey, *Memoirs of the Reign of George II* (1848) i. p. 298

He was indeed as false as his capacity would allow him to be, and was more capable in that walk than in any other, never having the least hesitation, from the principle or fear of future detection, in telling any lie that served his present purpose. He had a much weaker understanding, and, if possible, a more obstinate temper, than his father; that is, more tenacious of opinions he had once formed, though less capable of ever forming right ones. Had he had one grain of merit at the bottom of his heart, one should have had compassion for him in the situation to which his miserable poor head

[1] Morning receptions.

soon reduced him; for his case, in short, was this: he had a father that abhorred him, a mother that despised him, sisters that betrayed him, a brother set up against him, and a set of servants that neglected him, and were neither of use, nor capable of being of use to him, nor desirous of being so. . . .

✦

Sir Robert Walpole

i. *Source:* Lord Hervey, *Memoirs of the Reign of George II* (1848) i. pp. 22–5

Plate 3

He had a strength of parts equal to any advancement, a spirit to struggle with any difficulties, a steadiness of temper immoveable by any disappointments. He had great skill in figures, the nature of the funds, and the revenue; his first application was to this branch of knowledge; but as he afterwards rose to the highest posts of power, and continued longer there than any first minister in this country since Lord Burleigh ever did, he grew, of course, conversant with all the other parts of government, and very soon equally able in transacting them: the weight of the whole administration lay on him; every project was of his forming, conducting, and executing: from the time of making the Treaty of Hanover, all the foreign as well as domestic affairs passed through his hands: and, considering the little assistance he received from subalterns, it is incredible what a variety and quantity of business he dispatched; but as he had infinite application and long experience, so he had great method and a prodigious memory, with a mind and spirit that were indefatigable: and without every one of these natural as well as acquired advantages, it would indeed have been impossible for him to go through half what he undertook.

No man ever was blessed with a clearer head, a truer or quicker judgment, or a deeper insight into mankind; he knew the strength and weakness of everybody he had to deal with, and how to make his advantage of both; he had more warmth of affection and friendship for some particular people than one could have believed it possible for any one who had been so long raking in the dirt of mankind to be capable of feeling for so worthless a species of animals. One should naturally have imagined that the contempt and distrust he must have had for the species in gross, would have given him at least an indifference and distrust towards every particular. Whether his negligence of his enemies, and never stretching his power to gratify his resentment of the sharpest injury, was policy or constitution, I shall not determine: but I do not believe anybody who knows these times will deny that no minister ever was more outraged, or less apparently revengeful. Some of his friends, who were not unforgiving themselves, nor very apt to see imaginary faults in him, have condemned this easiness in his temper as a weakness that has often exposed him to new injuries, and given encouragement to his adversaries to insult him with impunity. . . .

In all occurrences, and at all times, and in all difficulties, he was constantly present and cheerful . . . no man ever knew better among those he had to deal with who was to be had, on what terms, by what methods, and how the acquisition would answer. He was not one of those projecting systematical great geniuses who are always thinking in theory, and are above common practice: he had been too long conversant in business not to know that in the fluctuation of human affairs and variety of accidents to which the best concerted schemes are liable, they must often be disappointed who build on the certainty of the most probable events; and therefore seldom turned his thoughts to the provisional warding off future evils which might or might not happen; or the scheming of remote advantages, subject to so many intervening crosses; but always applied himself to the present occurrence, studying and generally hitting upon the properest method to improve what was favourable, and the best expedient to extricate himself out of what was difficult. There never was any minister to whom access was so easy and so frequent, nor whose answers were more explicit. He knew how to oblige when he bestowed, and not to shock when he denied; to govern without oppressing, and conquer without triumph. He pursued his ambition without curbing his pleasures, and his pleasures without neglecting his business; he did the latter with ease, and indulged himself in the other without giving scandal or offence. In private life, and to all who had any dependence upon him, he was kind and indulgent; he was generous without ostentation, and an economist without penuriousness; not insolent in success, nor irresolute in distress; faithful to his friends and not inveterate to his foes.

ii. Lord Stair, speaking to Queen Caroline at the height of the Excise Crisis in April 1733, reveals his partisan bias.

Source: ibid. i. pp. 166–8

. . . 'But, Madam, though your Majesty knows nothing of this man but what he tells you himself, or what his creatures and flatterers, prompted by himself, tell you of him, yet give me leave to assure your Majesty that in no age, in no reign, in no country was ever any minister so universally odious as the man you support. He is hated by the army, because he is known to support them against his will, and hated by the country for supporting them at all; he is hated by the clergy, because they know the support they receive from him is policy, contrary to his principles of Whiggism, and a support he makes them earn at a dear rate; he is hated by the city of London, because he never did anything for the trading part of it, nor aimed at any interest of theirs but a corrupt influence over the directors and governors of the great monied companies; he is hated by all the Scotch to a man, because he is known to have combated every mark of favour the King has been so good to confer on any of that nation; and he is little better beloved by many Englishmen, even of those who vote with him and serve under him. His power being thus universally dreaded, and his measures being thus universally disliked, and your Majesty being thought his protectress, give me leave to say, Madam, the odium incurred by his oppressions and injustice is not entirely confined to his own person: and as everybody, Madam, does imagine that he cannot be so blind, so deaf, and so insensible as not to see, hear, and know himself obnoxious to the people of all ranks and denominations in the kingdom—so it is thought the only resource he now has is to throw power into the hands of the Crown, where he must take refuge, and from whence alone he can hope for protection. People are confirmed in this opinion by this enslaving scheme of Excises, which they neither do nor can think upon in any other light.

... That he absolutely governs your Majesty nobody doubts, and very few scruple to say; they own you have the appearance of power, and say you are contented with the appearance, whilst all the reality of power is his, derived from the King, conveyed through you, and vested in him. The King is looked upon as the engine of his minister's ambition, and your interest and influence over him as the secret springs by which this minister gives motion to all his master's actions.'

iii. Walpole's love of peace is emphasized here.

(a) *Source:* W. Coxe, *Memoirs of the Life and Administration of Sir Robert Walpole* (1798) i. p. 618

It is recorded that Sir Robert Walpole, hearing the bells ringing, enquired the cause of such rejoicing, and was informed that the bells were ringing for the declaration of war[1]. They now ring the bells, he replied, but they will soon wring their hands.

(b) *Source:* P. Yorke, *The Life and Correspondence of Philip Yorke, Earl of Hardwicke* (1913) i. p. 251

I [Newcastle] said then to him [Walpole], Lord Harrington present, 'When measures are agreed amongst us, it is very right that everybody should support them, but not to have the liberty of giving one's opinion before they are agreed, is very wrong.' He said shortly, 'What do you mean? The war[1] is yours, you have had the conduct of it, I wish you joy of it.'

❖

William Pulteney

Source: Lord Chesterfield, *Letters (with the Characters)* (1892) iii. pp. 1415–16

Plate 4 (a)

Mr Pulteney was formed by nature for social and convivial pleasures. Resentment made him engage in business. He had

[1] The War of Jenkins' Ear.

thought himself slighted by Sir Robert Walpole, to whom he publicly vowed not only revenge, but utter destruction. He had lively and shining parts, a surprising quickness of wit, and a happy turn to the most amusing and entertaining kinds of poetry, as epigrams, ballads, odes, etc.; in all which he had an uncommon facility. His compositions in that way were sometimes satirical, often licentious, but always full of wit.

He had a quick and clear conception of business, could equally detect and practise sophistry. He could state and explain the most intricate matters, even in figures, with the utmost perspicuity. His parts were rather above business; and the warmth of his imagination, joined to the impetuosity and restlessness of his temper, made him incapable of conducting it long together with prudence and steadiness.

He was a most complete orator and debater in the House of Commons; eloquent, entertaining, persuasive, strong, and pathetic, as occasion required; for he had arguments, wit, and tears, at his command. His breast was the seat of all those passions which degrade our nature and disturb our reason; there they raged in perpetual conflict; but *avarice*, the meanest of them all, generally triumphed, ruled absolutely, and in many instances, which I forbear to mention, most scandalously.

His sudden passion was outrageous, but supported by great personal courage. Nothing exceeded his ambition but his avarice; they often accompany, and are frequently and reciprocally the causes and the effects of each other; but the latter is always a clog upon the former. He affected good nature and compassion, and perhaps his heart might feel the misfortunes and distresses of his fellow-creatures, but his hand was seldom or never stretched out to relieve them. Though he was an able actor of truth and sincerity, he could occasionally lay them aside, to serve the purposes of his ambition or avarice.

He was once in the greatest point of view that ever I saw any subject in. When the Opposition, of which he was the leader in the House of Commons, prevailed at last against Sir Robert Walpole he became the arbiter between the Crown and the people; the former imploring his protection, the latter his support. In that critical moment his various jarring passions were in the highest ferment, and for a while suspended his ruling one. Sense of shame made him hesitate at turning courtier on a sudden, after having acted the patriot so long, and with so much applause; and his pride made him declare that he would accept of no place, vainly imagining that he could by such a simulated and temporary self-denial preserve his popularity with the public and his power at Court. He was mistaken in both. The King hated him almost as much for what he might have done, as for what he had done; and a motley Ministry was formed, which by no means desired his company. The nation looked upon him as a deserter, and he shrunk into insignificancy and an Earldom.

He made several attempts afterwards to retrieve the opportunity he had lost, but in vain; his situation would not allow it. He was fixed in the House of Lords, that hospital of incurables; and his retreat to popularity was cut off; for the confidence of the public, when once great and once lost, is never to be regained.

✦

John Carteret, Earl Granville

Source: Lord Chesterfield, *Letters (with the Characters)* (1892) iii. pp. 1418–19

Plate 4 (b)

Lord Granville had great parts, and a most uncommon share of learning for a man of quality. He was one of the best speakers in the House of Lords, both in the declamatory and the argumentative way. He had a wonderful quickness and precision in seizing the stress of a question, which no art, no sophistry, could disguise to him. In business he was bold, enterprising, and overbearing. He had been bred up in high monarchical, that is, tyrannical principles of government, which his ardent and imperious temper made him think were the only rational and practicable ones. He would have been a great First Minister in France, little inferior, perhaps, to Richelieu; in this government, which is yet free, he would have been a dangerous one, little less so, perhaps, than Lord St[r]afford. He was neither ill-natured nor vindictive, and had a great contempt for money. His ideas were all above it. In social life he was an agreeable, good-humoured, and instructive companion; a great but entertaining talker.

He degraded himself by the vice of drinking, which, together with a great stock of Greek and Latin, he brought away with him from Oxford, and retained and practised ever afterwards. By his own industry, he had made himself master of all the modern languages and had acquired a great knowledge of the law. His political knowledge of the interest of Princes and of commerce was extensive, and his notions were just and great. His character may be summed up, in nice precision, quick decision, and unbounded presumption.

❖

Henry Pelham

Source: Lord Chesterfield, *Letters (with the Characters)* (1892) iii. p. 1419

Plate 5 (a)

Mr Pelham had good sense, without either shining parts or any degree of literature. He had by no means an elevated or enterprising genius, but had a more manly and steady resolution than his brother the Duke of Newcastle. He had a gentlemanlike frankness in his behaviour, and as great a point of honour as a minister can have, especially a minister at the head of the Treasury, where numberless sturdy and indefatigable beggars of condition apply, who cannot all be gratified, nor all with safety be refused.

He was a very inelegant speaker in Parliament, but spoke with a certain candour and openness that made him be well heard, and generally believed.

He wished well to the public, and managed the finances with great care and personal purity. He was *par negotiis neque supra*; had many domestic virtues and no vices. If his place, and the power that accompanies it, made him some public enemies, his behaviour in both secured him from personal and rancorous ones. Those who wished him worst, only wished themselves in his place.

Upon the whole, he was an honourable man, and a well-wishing minister.

✦

The Duke of Newcastle

After 1751 Horace Walpole was opposed to the Pelhams for both personal and political reasons.

i. *Source:* H. Walpole, *Memoirs of the Reign of King George II* (1846) i. pp. 162–6

Plate 5 (b)

... He succeeded young to an estate of about £30,000 per annum, and to great influence and interest in several counties. This account in reality contains his whole character as a minister, for to the rest of his fortune he solely owed his every-other-way most unwarrantable elevation. ... His person was not naturally despicable; his incapacity, his mean soul, and the general low opinion of him, grew to make it appear ridiculous. A constant hurry in his walk, a restlessness of place, a borrowed importance, a real insignificance, gave him the perpetual air of a solicitor, though he was perpetually solicited; for he never conferred a favour till it was wrested from him, but often omitted that he most wished done. ... He had no pride but infinite self-love; jealousy was the great source of all his faults. ... There was no expense to which he was not addicted but generosity. ... His speeches in Council and Parliament were flowing and copious of words, but empty and unmeaning. ... He aimed at everything, endeavoured nothing. ... He was a Secretary of State without intelligence, a Duke without money, a man of infinite intrigue without secrecy or policy, a Minister despised and hated by his master, by all parties and ministers, without being turned out by any.

ii. *Source:* H. Walpole, *Letters* (ed. P. Cunningham, 1857-9) ii. p. 376

To Richard Bentley Esq.   Arlington St., March 17, 1754

... On Friday this august remnant of the Pelhams went to Court for the first time. At the foot of the stairs he cried and sunk down; the yeomen of the guard were forced to drag him up under the arms. When the closet-door opened, he flung himself at his length at the King's feet, sobbed, and cried, 'God bless your Majesty! God preserve your Majesty!' and lay there howling and embracing the King's knees, with one foot so extended, that my Lord Coventry, who was *luckily* in waiting, and begged the standers-by to retire, with—'For God's sake, gentlemen, don't look at a great man in distress,' endeavouring to shut the door, caught his Grace's foot, and made him roar out with pain.

iii. *Source: ibid.* iii. p. 362

To George Montagu Esq.   Arlington St., November 13, 1760

... This grave scene [the funeral of George II] was fully contrasted by the burlesque Duke of Newcastle. He fell into a fit of crying the moment he came into the chapel, and flung himself back into a stall, the Archbishop hovering over him with a smelling-bottle; but in two minutes his curiosity got the better of his hypocrisy, and he ran about the chapel with his glass to spy who was or was not there, spying with one hand, and mopping his eyes with the other. Then returned the fear of catching cold; and the Duke of Cumberland, who was sinking with heat, felt himself weighed down and turning round, found it was the Duke of Newcastle standing upon his train, to avoid the chill of the marble. ...

iv. *Source:* Lord Chesterfield, *Letters (with the Characters)* (1892) iii. pp. 1424-5

The public opinion put him below his level; for though he had no superior parts, or eminent talents, he had a most indefatigable industry, a perseverance, a Court craft, and a servile compliance with the will of his Sovereign for the time being; which qualities, with only a common share of common sense, will carry a man sooner and more safely through the dark labyrinths of a Court, than the most shining parts would do without those meaner talents.

He was good-natured to a degree of weakness, even to tears, upon the slightest occasions. Exceedingly timorous, both personally and politically, dreading the least innovation, and keeping with a scrupulous timidity in the beaten track of business as having the safest bottom.

I will mention one instance of this disposition, which I think will set it in its strongest light. When I brought the Bill into the House of Lords for correcting and amending the Calendar, I gave him previous notice of my intentions. He was alarmed at so bold an undertaking, and conjured me *not to stir matters* that had long been quiet; adding, that he did not love *New-fangled things*. I did not, however, yield to the cogency of these arguments, but brought in the Bill, and it passed unanimously. From such weaknesses it necessarily follows, that he could have no great ideas, nor elevation of mind.

His ruling, or rather his only, passion was the agitation, the bustle, and the hurry of business, to which he had been accustomed above forty years; but he was as dilatory in despatching it as he was eager to engage in it. He was always in a hurry, never walked, but always ran; insomuch that I have sometimes told him, that by his fleetness one should rather take him for the courier than the author of the letters.

He was as jealous of his power as an impotent lover of his mistress, without activity of mind enough to enjoy or exert it, but could not bear a share even in the appearances of it.

His levées were his pleasure, and his triumph; he loved to have them crowded, and consequently they were so. There he generally made people of business wait two or three hours in the ante-chamber, while he trifled away that time with some insignificant favourites in his closet. When at last he came into his levée-room, he accosted, hugged, embraced, and promised everybody, with a seeming cordiality, but at the same time with an illiberal and degrading familiarity.

He was exceedingly disinterested, very profuse of his own fortune, and abhorring all those means, too often used by persons in his station, either to gratify their avarice, or to supply their prodigality; for he retired from business in the year 1762, above four hundred thousand pounds poorer than when he first engaged in it.

Upon the whole, he was a compound of most human weaknesses, but unattainted with any vice or crime.

◆

William Pitt, Earl of Chatham

i. *Source:* H. Walpole, *Memoirs of the Reign of King George II* (1846) iii. pp. 84–6

Plate 6 (a)

Pitt was now arrived at undisturbed possession of that influence in affairs at which his ambition aimed, and which his presumption had made him flatter himself he could exert like those men of superior genius, whose talents have been called forth by some crisis to retrieve a sinking nation. He had said the last year to the Duke of Devonshire, 'My Lord, I am sure I can save this country, and no one else can.' It were ingratitude to him to say that he did not give such a reverberation to our stagnating Councils, as exceedingly altered the appearance of our fortune. He warded off the evil hour that seemed approaching; he infused vigour into our arms; he taught the nation to speak again as England used to speak to Foreign Powers; and so far from dreading invasions from France, he affected to turn us into invaders. Indeed, these efforts were so puny, so ill-concerted, so ineffectual to any essential purpose, that France looked down with scorn on such boyish flippancies, which Pitt deemed heroic, which Europe thought ridiculous, and which humanity saw were only wasteful of lives, and precedents of a more barbarous warfare than France had hitherto been authorized to carry on. In fact, Pitt had neither all the talents he supposed in himself, nor which he seemed to possess from the vacancy of great men around him. . . .

Pitt's was an unfinished greatness: considering how much of it depended on his words, one may almost call his an artificial greatness;

but his passion for fame and the grandeur of his ideas compensated for his defects. He aspired to redeem the honour of his country, and to place it in a point of giving law to nations. His ambition was to be the most illustrious man of the first country in Europe; and he thought that the eminence of glory could not be sullied by the steps to it being passed irregularly. He wished to aggrandize Britain in general, but thought not of obliging or benefiting individuals. . . .

ii. This speech, made upon his resignation in 1761, best reveals Pitt's proud and imperious nature.

Source: B. Williams, *The Life of William Pitt, Earl of Chatham* (1915) ii. pp. 112–13

'Without having ever asked any one single employment in my life, I was called by my Sovereign and by the Voice of the People to assist the State when others had abdicated the service of it. That being so no one can be surprised that I will go on no longer since my advice is not taken. . . . Being responsible I *will* direct, and will be responsible for nothing that I do not direct.'

iii. This account refers to Pitt in 1758.

Source: Earl Waldegrave, *Memoirs* (1821) pp. 15–17

Mr Pitt has the finest genius, improved by study and all the ornamental part of classical learning.

He came early into the House of Commons, where he soon distinguished himself; lost a cornetcy of horse, which was then his only subsistence; and in less than twenty years has raised himself to be First Minister, and the most powerful subject in this country.

He has a peculiar clearness and facility of expression; and has an eye as significant as his words. He is not always a fair or conclusive reasoner, but commands the passions with sovereign authority; and to inflame or captivate a popular assembly is a consummate orator. He has courage of every sort, cool or impetuous, active or deliberate.

At present he is the guide and champion of the people: whether he will long continue their friend seems somewhat doubtful. But if we may judge from his natural disposition, as it has hitherto shewn itself, his popularity and zeal for public liberty will have the same period: for he is imperious, violent, and implacable; impatient even of the slightest contradiction; and, under the mask of patriotism, has the despotic spirit of a tyrant.

However, though his political sins are black and dangerous, his private character is irreproachable; he is incapable of a treacherous or ungenerous action; and in the common offices of life is justly esteemed a man of veracity and a man of honour.

He mixes little in company, confining his society to a small junto of his relations, with a few obsequious friends, who consult him as an oracle, admire his superior understanding, and never presume to have an opinion of their own.

This separation from the world is not entirely owing to pride, or an unsociable temper; as it proceeds partly from bad health and a weak constitution. But he may find it an impassable barrier in the road of ambition; for though the mob can sometimes raise a minister, he must be supported by persons of higher rank, who may be mean enough in some particulars, yet will not be the patient followers of any man who despises their homage and avoids their solicitations. . . .

However, if Mr Pitt should maintain his power a few years, observation and experience may correct many faults, and supply many deficiencies: in the mean time, even his enemies must allow that he has the firmness and activity of a great minister; that he has hitherto conducted the war with spirit, vigour, and tolerable success; and though some favourite schemes may have been visionary and impracticable, they have at least been more honourable and less dangerous than the passive, unperforming pusillanimity of the late administration.

❖

Henry Fox, Lord Holland

Source: Earl Waldegrave, *Memoirs* (1821) p. 24
Plate 6 (b)

As to Fox, few men have been more unpopular; yet when I have asked his bitterest enemies what crimes they could allege against him, they always confined themselves to general accusation; that he was avaricious, encouraged jobs, had profligate friends, and dangerous connections; but never could produce a particular fact of any weight or consequence.

His warmth or impetuosity of temper led him into two very capital mistakes; he wantonly offended the Chancellor [Hardwicke] by personal reflections or ridicule in the affair of the Marriage Act: he also increased the number of his enemies by discovering an eagerness to be minister, whilst Mr Pelham was still alive: many of whose friends might possibly have attached themselves to him, if, instead of snatching at the succession, he had coolly waited till it had been delivered into his hands.

He has great parliamentary knowledge, but is rather an able debater than a complete orator; his best speeches are neither long nor premeditated; quick and concise replication is his peculiar excellence.

In business he is clear and communicative; frank and agreeable in society; and though he can pay his court on particular occasions, he has too much pride to flatter an enemy, or even a friend, where it is not necessary.

Upon the whole, he has some faults, but more good qualities; is a man of sense and judgement, notwithstanding some indiscretion; and with small allowances for ambition, party, and politics, is a warm friend, a man of veracity, and a man of honour.

❧

George III

This description of George was given by Earl Waldegrave (his governor from 1752–6) before his accession.

Source: Earl Waldegrave, *Memoirs* (1821) pp. 8–10

Plate 7 (a)

The Prince of Wales is entering into his 21st year, and it would be unfair to decide upon his character in the early stages of life, when there is so much time for improvement.

His parts, though not excellent, will be found very tolerable, if ever they are properly exercised.

He is strictly honest, but wants that frank and open behaviour which makes honesty appear amiable.

When he had a very scanty allowance, it was one of his favourite maxims that men should be just before they are generous: his income is now very considerably augmented, but his generosity has not increased in equal proportion.

His religion is free from all hypocrisy, but is not of the most charitable sort; he has rather too much attention to the sins of his neighbour.

He has spirit, but not of the active kind; and does not want resolution, but it is mixed with too much obstinacy.

He has great command of his passions, and will seldom do wrong, except when he mistakes wrong for right; but as often as this shall happen, it will be difficult to undeceive him, because he is uncommonly indolent, and has strong prejudices.

His want of application and aversion to business would be far less dangerous, was he eager in the pursuit of pleasure; for the transition from pleasure to business is both shorter and easier than from a state of total inaction.

He has a kind of unhappiness in his temper, which, if it be not conquered before it has taken too deep a root, will be a source of frequent anxiety. Whenever he is displeased, his anger does not break out with heat and violence; but he becomes sullen and silent, and retires to his closet; not to compose his mind by study or contemplation, but merely to indulge the melancholy enjoyment of his own ill humour. Even when the fit is ended, unfavourable symptoms very frequently return, which indicate that on certain occasions his Royal Highness has too correct a memory.

Though I have mentioned his good and bad qualities, without flattery, and without aggravation, allowance should still be made, on account of his youth, and his bad education: for though the Bishop of Peterborough, now Bishop of Salisbury, the preceptor; Mr Stone, the sub-governor; and Mr Scott, the sub-preceptor, were men of sense, men of learning, and worthy, good men, they had but little weight and influence. The mother and the nursery always prevailed.

During the course of the last year, there has, indeed, been some alteration; the authority of the nursery has gradually declined, and the Earl of Bute, by the assistance of the mother, has now the entire confidence. But whether this change will be greatly to his Royal Highness's advantage, is a nice question, which cannot hitherto be determined with any certainty.

❖

The Earl of Bute

Source: Lord Chesterfield, *Letters (with the Characters)* (1892) iii. pp. 1431–5

Plate 7 (b)

Here the new scene opened [the accession of George III]: Lord Bute arrived from the greatest favour to the highest power and took no care to dissemble or soften either, in the eyes of the public, who always look upon them with envy and malignity; but on the contrary, avowed them both openly. He interfered in every thing, disposed of every thing, and undertook every thing, much too soon for his inexperience in business, and for at best his systematic notions of it, which are seldom or never reducible to practice. I would not be understood by this to blame Lord Bute, no; I lay the blame more justly upon human nature. Let us consider him as a private man, of a very small patrimonial estate, passing the greatest part of his life in silence and obscurity, never engaged in any business, and little practised in the ways and characters of men, at once raised to the highest pitch of favour and power, and governing three kingdoms. And then say whose head would not turn with so sudden and universal a change? Every man who is new in business is at first either too rash or too timorous; but he was both. He undertook what he feared to execute, and what consequently he executed ill.

His intentions for the King and the public were certainly honest and constitutional, as appeared by the first three acts of his administration, which were, inducing the King to demand a certain rentcharge for his Civil List, so that the public might know with certainty what he received, which was not the case in the former reign; his endeavouring to extinguish the odious names of Whigs and Tories, by taking off the proscription under which the latter, who are at least one-half of the nation, had too long and too unjustly groaned; and lastly, by procuring an Act of Parliament to make the places of the Judges for life, notwithstanding the demise of the Crown. But these right and popular acts availed him nothing, and that chiefly because he had the power of doing them; the popular run was strong against him, which was artfully fomented by the ministers of the former reign, whom he had either displaced, or at least stripped of their power.

If ever the multitude deviate into the right, it is always for the wrong reason, as appeared upon this occasion; for the great cry against Lord Bute was upon account of his being a Scotchman, the only fault which he could not possibly correct. When the King came to the Crown he was his Groom of the Stole, and would have done more prudently if he had continued some time in that post; but he was too impatient to shine in the full meridian of his power. He made himself immediately Secretary of State, Knight of the Garter and Privy Purse; he gave an English peerage to his wife; and the reversion of a very lucrative employment for life to his eldest son. He placed and displaced whom he pleased; gave peerages without number, and pensions without bounds; by these means he proposed to make his ground secure for the permanency of his power; for his favour he did not doubt of, nor had he the least reason; but unfortunately for him, he had made no personal friends: this was partly owing to his natural temper, which was dry, unconciliatory and sullen, with great mixture of pride. He never looked at those he spoke to, or who spoke to him, a great fault in a minister, as in the general opinion of mankind it implies conscious guilt; besides that, if it hinders him from being penetrated, it equally hinders him from penetrating others. The subaltern ministers whom he employed under him, particularly in the management of the House of Commons, were most of them incapable of serving him, and the others unwilling to do it. No man living had his entire confidence; and no man thinks himself bound by a half confidence. He opened his administration with negotiating or rather asking a peace of

France; and said imprudently enough to many people *that he would make one. . . .*

. . . When the peace was thus concluded, Lord Bute thought himself firmly established: he got it approved of by a great majority in both Houses. In the House of Lords he himself triumphed in the share which he owned he had in it, and imprudently and theatrically declared, that he desired no more glorious epitaph to be engraved on his tomb-stone. But the peace gave him not the strength he expected; on the contrary, it added to the mass of his unpopularity. The nation universally condemned it, not upon knowledge but because it was made by a favourite, and a Scotsman, two inexpiable sins in the opinion, or rather in the humour, of an English multitude. The truth is, that the peace was not so bad as it was represented by some, and believed by most people; nor was it so good as it ought to have been and certainly might have been, if more time and better abilities had been employed in negotiating it. It must be allowed to have been inadequate to our successes in the war; and, in my opinion, the whole cast and shape of it were wrong.

In the mean time, Lord Bute had placed himself at the head of the Treasury, from whence he had shoved the Duke of Newcastle, as he had also Mr Pitt and Lord Temple, from their posts of Secretary of State and Privy Seal; and had formed a ministry of his own creation, but without placing any real confidence in them, or they in him. He placed, displaced, and shifted the places of his subalterns, without selecting or trusting those who were the fittest for them. He placed Mr Fox, whom he both hated and distrusted, at the head of the House of Commons. He was both able and experienced in that business, but knew very well that he owed that preference to Lord Bute's necessity, and not to his choice; on the other hand, Lord Bute feared Mr Fox's ability, and remembered the fable of the Horse and the Man; therefore, though he had seemingly trusted him with the management of the House of Commons, his real confidence was placed in some of his inferior and insufficient creatures, those who occasionally opposed Mr Fox. This disgusted Mr Fox so much, that at the end of the session he insisted upon going into the House of Lords, which Lord Bute most willingly agreed to.

In that same session, amongst the Ways and Means to raise the supplies of the year, an excise was laid upon cyder; though the thing was right, the name was odious; and Lord Bute, if he had had more experience, and known the temper of the people, would have known, that even right things cannot be done at all times, especially at that dawn of his administration. This scheme was imputed wholly to him, and filled the measure of his unpopularity. He was burnt in effigy in all the cyder counties, hissed and insulted in the streets of London. It is natural to suppose, and it is undoubtedly true, that the Opposition, which consisted in general of persons of the greatest rank, property, and experience in business, enjoyed and increased this unpopularity to the utmost of their power; and accordingly it was carried to an alarming height. Lord Bute, who had hitherto appeared a presumptuous, now appeared to be a very timorous minister, characters by no means inconsistent, for he went about the streets timidly and disgracefully, attended at a small distance by a gang of *bruisers*, who are the scoundrels and ruffians that attend the Bear Gardens, and who would have been but a poor security to him against the dangers he apprehended from the whole of London.

In this odd situation, unpopular without guilt, fearing without danger, presumptuous without resolution, and proud without being respectable, or respected, he on a sudden, and to the universal surprise of the public, quitted his post of First Commissioner of the Treasury, and pretended to retire for ever from business and enjoy the comforts of private and social life; but he neither intended to quit his real power nor personal favour with the King which he was in all events secure of, and proposed to rule, as it is commonly called, behind the curtain. Accordingly he delegated his ministry, but without his power, to Mr Grenville, his successor in the Treasury, who talked over business very copiously, but with great inutility in dispatch of it; to Lord Egremont, Secretary of State, who was proud, self-sufficient, but incapable; and to Lord Halifax, the other Secretary of State, who had parts, application, and personal disinterestedness. These were called the Triumvirate; and Lord Bute declared, that the King had placed his administration wholly in their hands: they thought so themselves for a time, because they wished it, but the public never thought so one moment; and looked still at Lord Bute through the curtain, which indeed was a very transparent one.

❖

The Marquis of Rockingham

While Rockingham was indeed inadequate as a politician, Walpole here, as elsewhere, is more than a little biased.

Source: H. Walpole, *Memoirs of the Reign of George III* (1851) ii. p. 197

Plate 8 (a)

More childish in his deportment than in his age, he was totally void of all information. Ambitious, with excessive indolence; fond of talking of business, but dilatory in the execution; his single talent lay in attracting dependants: yet, though proud and self-sufficient, he had almost as many governors as dependants. To this unpromising disposition, he had so weak a frame of person and nerves, that no exigence could surmount his timidity of speaking in public; and having been only known to that public by his passion for horse-races, men could not be cured of their surprise at seeing him First Minister, as he never could give them an opportunity of knowing whether he had any other talents. A silent First Minister was a phenomenon unknown since Parliaments had borne so great a share in the revolutions of government. His personal character was blameless—unfortunately, the time required something more than negative qualities.

❖

Lord North

Source: H. Walpole, *Memoirs of the Reign of George III* (1851) iv. pp. 78–83

Plate 8 (b)

Frederick, Lord North, eldest son of the Earl of Guilford, was now in the thirty-eighth year of his age. Nothing could be more coarse or clumsy or ungracious than his outside. Two large prominent eyes that rolled about to no purpose (for he was utterly short-sighted), a wide mouth, thick lips, and inflated visage, gave him the air of a blind trumpeter. A deep untuneable voice, which, instead of modulating, he enforced with unnecessary pomp, a total neglect of his person, and ignorance of every civil attention, disgusted all who judge by appearance, or withhold their approbation till it is courted. But within that rude casket were enclosed many useful talents. He had much wit, good humour, strong natural sense, assurance and promptness, both of conception and elocution. His ambition had seemed to aspire to the height, yet he was not very ambitious. He was thought interested, yet was not avaricious. What he did, he did without a mask, and was not delicate in choosing his means. He had lent himself readily to all the violences of Mr Grenville against Wilkes, had seized the moment of advancement by accepting the post of Chancellor of the Exchequer ... when the Court wanted a person to oppose to the same Mr Grenville; and with equal alacrity had served under the Duke of Grafton. When the first post became vacant by the Duke's strange retreat, no man so ready to place himself in the gap as Lord North. It was in truth worth his ambition, though he should rule but a day, to attain the rank of Prime Minister. He had knowledge, and though fond of his amusement, seemed to have all the necessary activity till he reached the summit. Yet that industry ceased when it became most requisite. He had neither system, nor principles, nor shame, sought neither the fame of the Crown or of the people, but enjoyed the good luck of fortune with a gluttonous epicurism that was equally careless of glory and disgrace. His indolence prevented his forming any plan. His indifference made him leap from one extreme to another; and his insensibility to reproach reconciled him to any contradiction. ... If he had ambition it was of very mean complexion, for he stooped to be but a nominal Prime Minister, and suffered the King's private junto to enjoy the whole credit of favour, while, between submission and laziness, Lord North himself was seldom the author of the measures in which he bore the principal part. This passive and inglorious tractability, and his being connected with no faction, made him welcome to the King: his having no predominant fault or vice recommended him to the nation, and his good humour

43

and wit to everybody but to the few whom his want of good breeding and attention offended. One singularity came out in his character, which was, that no man was more ready for extremes under the administration of others, no man more temperate than Lord North during his own: in effect, he was a man whom few hated, fewer could esteem. As a minister he had no foresight, no consistence, no firmness, no spirit. He miscarried in all he undertook in America, was more improvident than unfortunate, less unfortunate than he deserved to be. If he was free from vices, he was as void of virtues; and it is a paltry eulogium of a Prime Minister of a great country, yet the best that can be allotted to Lord North, that, though his country was ruined under his administration, he preserved his good humour and neither felt for his country nor for himself.

❧

Edmund Burke

Source: Sir N. W. Wraxall, *Historical Memoirs of My Own Time* (1884) ii. pp. 26–36

Plate 9 (a)

If Fox occupied the first place in the ranks of Opposition, Burke might be pronounced the second in that powerful body. His endowments of mind superseded every defect of birth, fortune, connections, or country, and placed him on an eminence to which no subject in my time, unassisted by those advantages, with the single exception of Sheridan, has ever attained in the public estimation. For it may be justly questioned whether the splendid talents of the first Mr Pitt would have forced his way into the Cabinet unaided and unsustained by his alliance with the family of Grenville, though his own paternal descent was most honourable. Of years much more advanced than Fox, Burke had already attained to the acme of his fame as an orator, and could not well augment the reputation which he had acquired in that capacity. Perhaps if we were to point out the period of his life when he stood on the highest ground as a public man in the estimation of all parties, we should name the year 1781....

... He was then more than fifty years of age, of which he had passed fifteen in the House of Commons....

... Nature had bestowed on him a boundless imagination, aided by a memory of equal strength and tenacity. His fancy was so vivid that it seemed to light up by its own powers, and to burn without consuming the aliment on which it fed; sometimes bearing him away into ideal scenes created by his own exuberant mind, but from which he sooner or later returned to the subject of debate, descending from his most aerial flights by a gentle and imperceptible gradation till he again touched the ground. Learning waited on him like a handmaid, presenting to his choice all that antiquity had culled or invented most elucidatory of the topic under discussion. He always seemed to be oppressed under the load and variety of his intellectual treasures, of which he frequently scattered portions with a lavish hand to inattentive, impatient, ignorant, hungry, and sleepy auditors, undeserving of such presents. Nor did he desist, though warned by the clamorous vociferation of the House to restrain or to abbreviate his speeches. Every power of oratory was wielded by him in turn, for he could be during the same evening, often within the space of a few minutes, pathetic and humorous, acrimonious and conciliating, now giving loose to his indignation or severity, and then, almost in the same breath, calling to his assistance wit and ridicule....

... His personal qualities of temper and disposition by no means corresponded with his intellectual endowments. Throughout his general manner and deportment in Parliament there was a mixture of petulance, impatience, and at times of intractability, which obscured the lustre of his talents. His features and the undulating motions of his head while under the influence of anger or passion were eloquently expressive of this irritability, which on some occasions seemed to approach towards alienation of mind. Even his friends could not always induce him to listen to reason and remonstrance, though they sometimes held him down in his seat by the skirts of his coat in order to prevent the ebullitions of his violence or indignation. Gentle, mild, and amenable to argument in private society, of which he formed the delight and the ornament, he was often intemperate and reprehensibly personal in Parliament. Fox, however irritated, never forgot that he was a chief. Burke, in his most sublime flights, was only a partisan. The countenance of the latter, full of intellect but destitute of softness, which rarely relaxed into a smile, did not invite approach or conciliation. His enmities and prejudices, though they originated in principle as well as in conviction, yet became tinged with the virulent spirit of party, and were eventually in many instances inveterate, unjust, and insurmountable. Infinitely more respectable than Fox, he was nevertheless far less amiable. Exempt from his defects and irregularities, Burke wanted the suavity of Fox's manner, his amenity, and his placability. The one procured admirers, the other possessed friends. . . .

❖

The Earl of Shelburne

Source: Sir N. W. Wraxall, *Historical Memoirs of My Own Time* (1884) ii. pp. 62–3

Plate 9 (b)

In his person, manners, and address, the Earl of Shelburne wanted no external quality requisite to captivate or conciliate mankind. Affable, polite, communicative, and courting popularity, he drew round him a number of followers or adherents. His personal courage was indisputable. Spendid and hospitable at his table, he equally delighted his guests by the charms of his conversation and society. In his magnificent library, one of the finest of its kind in England, he could appear as a philosopher and a man of letters. With such various endowments of mind, sustained by rank and fortune, he necessarily excited universal consideration, and seemed to be pointed out by nature for the first employments. But the confidence which his moral character inspired did not equal the reputation of his abilities. His adversaries accused him of systematic duplicity and insincerity. They even asserted that unless all the rules of physiognomy were set at defiance, his very countenance and features eloquently indicated falsehood. In order to fix upon him so injurious an imputation, they gave him the epithet of Malagrida, from the name of a Portuguese Jesuit well known in the modern history of that kingdom. And these insinuations, though not perhaps accompanied with proofs, were nevertheless, either from the credulity or from the malignity of mankind, widely circulated, as well as very generally believed throughout the nation.

❖

Robert, Lord Clive

Source: C. Caraccioli, *Life of Robert Lord Clive* (1775) i. pp. 13, 466–8

Plate 10 (a)

I. It was early in the Spring, in the year 1743, that young Clive sailed for the East Indies, he was then in the eighteenth year of his age, a time when the genius and the imagination of most young men portend the exertion of their talents in riper years.

He had neither personal accomplishments, nor endearing qualities that could prepossess either sex in his favour, he was short, inclined to be corpulent, awkward, and unmannerly; his aspect was gloomy, sullen, and forbidding: his temper morose and intractable: his apprehension dull, and his mind unadorned by classical knowledge, tho' he seemed averse to the drudgery and confinement of a country house: all the time he was employed in that servile capacity, his companions did not perceive that he had other views and military talents, till he shewed them in the field. . . .

II. Indeed he was a man of business to all intents and purposes, of great application and activity. The climate of Bengal agreed extremely well with his lordship's constitution, and the temperance he observed in his diet was conducive to the health he enjoyed, notwithstanding the vicissitudes of it; he was commonly an early riser, and devoted part of the morning to business; after breakfast he used to take some exercise in the palankeen[1] or in a carriage, and a few select friends of his select committee or some other senior

[1] Covered litter for one person.

servants of his company dined with him. His table was served with delicacy and profusion, and all the most exquisite wines of Europe were at the discretion of his guests. If he was in good humour, he would encourage a free circulation of the bottle, and by intervals stimulate mirth and jollity; but he soon relapsed in his natural pensive mood, and was after silent for a considerable time. His conversation was not lively, but rational and solid. As he seldom drank freely enough to be seen without disguise, he was impenetrable, except to a few confidants to whom he entrusted the execution of his schemes and designs. It was not often that his guests were allowed a great latitude of freedom, as he was always stately and commonly reserved. After dinner he took sometimes a little repose, as it is customary in this torrid region. Towards the evening, he resorted to some gardens with a few companions, and after supper either played at cards, of which he was fond in select company, or retired with some favourite woman. It cannot be said that he enjoyed life, he only varied these fashionable amusements which gave him no real pleasure or satisfaction. Since he had been obliged by his rank in life to converse with ministers and statesmen, he had applied himself to politics, and in reading books that might give him some useful knowledge of the English constitution. He was not an orator but he spoke with propriety and judgement. His style as may be seen in his letters, was neither elevated nor contemptible. He was perfectly well acquainted with the genius of the Asiatics, and nobody knew better how to take advantage of their apprehensions and pusillanimity. . . .

✦

Warren Hastings

Source: State Papers of the Governors-General of India (ed. G. W. Forrest, 1910) i. pp. 318–20

Plate 10 (b)

(a) In their address the inhabitants of Benares stated: 'He laid the foundations of justice and the pillars of the law. In every shape, we, the inhabitants of this country, during the time of his administration, lived in ease and peace. We are therefore greatly satisfied with and thankful to him. As the said Mr Hastings was long acquainted with the modes of government in these regions, so the inmost purpose of his heart was openly and secretly, indeed, bent upon those things which might maintain inviolate our religious advances and persuasions, and guard us in even the minutest respect from misfortune and calamity. In every way he cherished us in honour and credit.'

(b) The Pundits and other Brahmins of Benares sent him an address in which they wrote: 'Whenever that man of vast reason, the Governor-General, Mr Hastings, returned to this place, and people of all ranks were assembled at that time he gladdened the heart of everyone by his behaviour, which consisted of kind wishes and agreeable conversation, expressions of compassion for the distressed, acts of politeness, and a readiness to relieve and protect everyone alike without distinction. To please us dull people, he caused a spacious music gallery to be built at his own expense, over the gateway of the temple of Beesmaswar, which is esteemed the head jewel of all places of holy visitation. He never at any time, nor on any occasion, either by neglecting to promote the happiness of the people, or by looking with the eye of covetousness, displayed an inclination to distress any individual whatsoever.'

(c) The inhabitants of Moorshedabad also forwarded an address, in which they stated 'the whole period of Mr Hastings' residence in this country exhibited his good conduct towards the inhabitants. No oppression nor tyranny was admitted over any one. He observed the rules of respect and attention to ancient families. He did not omit the performances of the duties of politeness and civility towards all men of rank and station when an interview took place with them. In affairs concerning the government and revenues, he was not covetous of other men's money and property; he was not open to bribery. He restricted the farmers and officers in their oppressions in a manner that prevented them from exercising that tyranny which motives of self-interest and private gain might instigate them to observe towards the ryots[1] and helpless. He used great exertions to cultivate the country, to increase the

[1] Indian peasants.

agriculture and the revenues without deceit, and with perfect propriety and rectitude. He respected the learned and wise men, and for the propagation of learning he built a college, and endowed it with a provision for the maintenance of the students, insomuch that thousands reaping the benefits thereof offer up their prayers for the prosperity of England, and for the success of the Company.'

❖

Edmund Gibson, Bishop of London

This portrait shows only the unfavourable side of Gibson, who was, in fact, one of the best of the early eighteenth-century bishops.

Source: Hist. MSS. Comm., Diary of the 1st Earl of Egmont i. p. 444

21 November, 1733

We then talked of other things, and particularly the character of some Bishops. That the Bishop of London is ambitious and loves power, and has nineteen Bishops at Command, who do everything he would have them, which will secure his being Archbishop of Canterbury, but at the same time, not willing to disoblige the ministry, he is not active to suppress Popery, nor to encourage men of learning and zeal for the Church, because they will not be tools. That when he waited on him to acquaint him with the great number of Protestants converted to Popery daily, and to desire, as he was a Privy Councillor, he would endeavour the laws against Popish regulars should be put in execution, there being no pretence to connive at the number of them now in England, who have no business here, seeing the secular priests are sufficient to say Mass, and confess the Popish laity, the Bishop shrugged his shoulders and said he had spoke of it, but the Ministry would not hear him for fear of disobliging Cardinal Fleury.

❖

John Wesley

Source: J. Hampson, *Memoirs of the late Rev. John Wesley* (1791)
iii. pp. 166–9, 178–80
Plate 11 (a)

The figure of Mr Wesley was remarkable. His stature was of the lowest: his habit of body in every period of life, the reverse of corpulent, and expressive of strict temperance, and continual exercise and notwithstanding his small size, his step was firm, and his appearance, till within a few years of his death, vigorous and muscular. His face, for an old man, was one of the finest we have seen. A clear, smooth forehead, an aquiline nose, an eye the brightest and most piercing that can be conceived, and a freshness of complexion, scarcely ever to be found at his years, and impressive of the most perfect health, conspired to render him a venerable and interesting figure. Few have seen him, without being struck with his appearance: and many, who have been greatly prejudiced against him, have been known to change their opinions, the moment they were introduced into his presence. In his countenance, and demeanour, there was a cheerfulness mingled with gravity; a sprightliness which was the natural result of an unusual flow of spirits, and was yet accompanied with every mark of the most serene tranquillity. His aspect, particularly in profile, had a strong character of acuteness and penetration.

In dress, he was a pattern of neatness and simplicity. A narrow, pleated stock, a coat with a small upright collar, no buckles at his knees, no silk or velvet in any part of his apparel, and a head as white as snow, gave an idea of something primitive and apostolical: while an air of neatness and cleanliness was diffused over his whole person.

His rank, as a preacher, is pretty generally understood. His attitude in the pulpit was graceful and easy; his action calm and natural, yet pleasing and expressive: his voice not loud but clear and manly; his style neat, simple, perspicuous: and admirably adapted to the capacity of his hearers. . . .

His manner, in private life, was the reverse of cynical or forbidding. It was sprightly and pleasant, to the last degree; and presented a beautiful contrast to the austere deportment of many of his preachers and people, who seem to have ranked laughter among the mortal sins. It was impossible to be long in his company, without partaking his hilarity. . . .

A remarkable feature in Mr Wesley's character, was his placability. His temper was naturally warm and impetuous. Religion had, in a great degree, corrected this; though it was by no means eradicated. Generally indeed, he preserved an air of sedateness and tranquillity, which formed a striking contrast to the liveliness, so conspicuous in all his actions. Persecution from without, he bore not only without anger, but without the least apparent emotion. But it was not the case in contests of another kind. Opposition from his preachers or people he could never brook. His authority he held sacred and, when that was called in question, we have known him repeatedly transported into a high degree of indignation. But what he said of himself was strictly true. He had a great facility in forgiving injuries. Submission, on the part of an offender, presently disarmed his resentment, and he would treat him with great kindness and cordiality.

❖

Samuel Johnson

Source: James Boswell, *The Life of Samuel Johnson* (1826) iv. p. 419
Plate 11 (b)

His figure was large and well formed, and his countenance of the cast of an ancient statue; yet his appearance was rendered strange and somewhat uncouth, by conclusive cramps, by the scars of that distemper which it was once imagined the royal touch could cure, and by a slovenly mode of dress. He had the use only of one eye; yet so much does mind govern and even supply the deficiency of organs, that his visual perceptions, as far as they extended, were uncommonly quick and accurate. So morbid was his temperament that he never knew the natural joy of a free and vigorous use of his limbs: when he walked, it was like the struggling gait of one in fetters; when he rode, he had no command or direction of his horse, but was carried as if in a balloon. . . .

He was a sincere and zealous Christian, of high Church of England and monarchical principles, which he would not tamely suffer to be questioned; and had, perhaps, at an early period, narrowed his mind somewhat too much, both as to religion and politics. . . . He was steady and inflexible in maintaining the obligations of religion and morality; both from a regard for the order of society, and from a veneration for the GREAT SOURCE of all order; correct, nay stern in his taste; hard to please, and easily offended; impetuous and irritable in his temper, but of the most humane and benevolent heart, which shewed itself not only in a most liberal charity, as far as his circumstances would allow, but in a thousand instances of active benevolence. . . . As he was general and unconfined in his studies, he cannot be considered as master of any one particular science; but he had accumulated a vast and various collection of learning and knowledge, which was so arranged in his mind, as to be ever in readiness to be brought forth. But his superiority over other learned men consisted chiefly in what may be called the art of thinking, the art of using his mind; a certain continual power of seizing the useful substance of all that he knew, and exhibiting it in a clear and forceful manner; so that knowledge, which we often see to be no better than lumber in men of dull understanding, was, to him, true, evident, and actual wisdom . . . He had accustomed himself to such accuracy in his common conversation, that he at all times expressed his thoughts with great force, and an eloquent choice of language, the effect of which was aided by his having a loud voice, and a slow deliberate utterance. In him were united a most logical head with a most fertile imagination, which gave him an extraordinary advantage in arguing; for he could reason close or wide, as he saw best for the moment. Exulting in his intellectual strength and dexterity, he could, when he pleased, be the greatest sophist that ever contended in the lists of declamation; and from a spirit of contradiction and a delight in shewing his powers, he would often maintain the wrong side with equal warmth and ingenuity; so that when there was an audience, his real opinions could seldom be gathered from his talk; though when he was in company with a single friend, he could discuss a subject with genuine fairness; but he was too conscientious to make error permanent and pernicious by deliberately writing it; and, in all his numerous works, he earnestly inculcated what appeared to him to be the truth; his piety being constant, and the ruling principle of all his conduct.

Such was Samuel Johnson, a man whose talents, acquirements, and virtues, were so extraordinary, that the more his character is considered, the more he will be regarded by the present age, and by posterity, with admiration and reverence.

POLITICAL
and
CONSTITUTIONAL

The Eighteenth Century Constitution

I. RELATIONS BETWEEN KING AND MINISTERS

i. *Lord Orford is here writing to advise his friend and pupil, Henry Pelham—20 October, 1743*

Source: W. Coxe, *Memoirs of the Administration of the Rt. Hon. Henry Pelham* (1829) i. pp. 104–5

This leads me to the most tender and delicate part of the whole; I mean your behaviour, and your manner of treating this subject with him [the King]. It is a great misfortune, that you have not time; for time and address have often carried things, that met at first onset, with great reluctance; and you must expect to meet the King instructed, and greatly prepared in favour of the points which Carteret has in view to drive. Address and management are the weapons you must fight and defend with: plain truths will not be relished at first, in opposition to prejudices, conceived and infused in favour of his own partialities; and you must dress up all you offer, with the appearance of no other view or tendency, but to promote his service in his own way, to the utmost of your power. And the more you can make anything appear to be his own, and agreeable to his declaration and orders, given to you before he went, the better you will be heard: as, the power to treat with such persons, as should be necessary to carry on his service in your own hands; the encouragement and hopes to be given to the Whigs, by you, as arising from himself. Hint, at first, the danger he will run, in deviating from his own rule; shew him the unavoidable necessity there will be, of dissolving this Parliament, if he departs from the body of the Whigs; and let him see the consequences of going to a new election, in the height of the war, which will certainly end in a rank Tory Parliament, that will at once put a stop to all the measures that are now in practice, and for ever defeat all his views and desires, which are made the pretences to him, of hazarding the change.

ii. *The Duke of Newcastle to Lord Chesterfield—22 February, 1745*
   Source: Add. MS. 32804, ff. 231-2

You are certainly in the right, that many things, to, and from, foreign Courts, are convey'd through . . . channels, unknown to us. And most of the material foreign ministers are as much attach'd to a certain person [Granville], and act as much in concert with him, as formerly: and, what is worse, I am afraid, that is not only known, but approved, and done in concert with somebody else [the King]: the time will come, and that soon, when all that must be explain'd. The King's servants must be his ministers, exclusive of all others; or they cannot remain his servants.

iii. *Horace Walpole refers to the difficulties at the beginning of the Broadbottom administration*
   Source: H. Walpole, *Letters* (ed. P. Cunningham, 1857-9) i. pp. 334-5

To Horace Mann Esq.   Arlington St., December 24, 1744

. . . the King, instigated by Lord Granville, has used all his ministry as ill as possible, and has with the greatest difficulty been brought to consent to the necessary changes. . . . It is not easy to say where power resides at present: it is plain that it resides not in the King; and yet he has enough to hinder anyone else from having it. His new governors have no interest with him—scarce any converse with him.

iv. *Minute from the ministers*
   This minute was drawn up, presumably for presentation to the King, by the ministers whom he was forced to reinstate in February 1746.
   Source: Add. MS. 35870 f. 117

That, out of duty to the King, and regard to the public, it is apprehended that His Majesty's late servants cannot return into his service, without being honoured, with that degree of authority, confidence, and credit from His Majesty, which the ministers of the Crown have usually enjoy'd in this country, and which is absolutely necessary for carrying on his service. That His Majesty will be pleased entirely to withdraw his confidence and countenance from those persons, who of late have, behind the curtain, suggested private councils, with the view of creating difficulties to his servants, who are responsible for everything, whilst those persons are responsible for nothing.

That His Majesty will be pleased to demonstrate his conviction of mind that those persons have deceiv'd or misled him, by representing that they had sufficient credit and interest in the nation to support and carry on the public affairs, and that he finds they are not able to do it. . . .

That he will be graciously pleased to perfect the scheme lately humbly proposed to him for bringing Mr Pitt into some honourable employment, and also the other persons formerly named with him. . . .

v. *George III to the Prince of Wales*

George III wrote (in March 1783) to the Prince of Wales when faced by the possibility of the Fox-North coalition. The letter was in fact never sent.

Source: Windsor MSS, Geo. 41795

The situation of the times are such that I must, if I attempt to carry on the business of the nation, give up every political principle on which I have acted, which I should think very unjustifiable, as I have always attempted to act agreeable to my duty; and must form a ministry from among men who know I cannot trust them and therefore will not accept office without making me a kind of slave; this undoubtedly is a cruel dilemma, and leaves me but one step to take without the destruction of my principles and honour; the resigning my Crown, my dear Son to you, quitting this my native country for ever and ever and returning to the dominions of my forefathers.

Your difficulties will not be the same. You have never been in a situation to form any political system, therefore, are open to adopt what the times may make necessary; and no set of men can ever have offended you or made it impossible for you to employ them.

i. *Spanish Depredations on English Shipping*

The Spanish depredations upon English shipping in the New World were being debated in the Commons in 1738; this extract is taken from a speech by Mr Pulteney.

Source: Parliamentary History of England x. p. 591

We have in this kingdom several councils; we have a privy council; a cabinet council; and for what I know, a more secret and less numerous council still, by which the other two are directed: but the Parliament is his Majesty's great and chief council: it is the council which all ministers ought both for their own sakes and their masters, to advise his Majesty to consult with, upon every affair of great weight and importance; for, from all our histories we shall find, that those kings have been the most happy and glorious, who have often consulted with their Parliaments; and that those ministers have always gone through their administration with the greatest ease and applause, and have divested themselves of their power with the greatest safety to themselves, which seldom happens to any but those who have advised their masters to depend chiefly upon the advice of their Parliaments.

In our privy council, Sir, in our cabinet council, and in any more secret council, if there be any such, the Hon. gentleman [Sir Robert Walpole] may be supposed to have a sway; nay, it may be even suspected that he has, under his Majesty, the chief direction of each; and therefore he may, some time hereafter, be made to answer for their determinations; but it cannot be suspected that he has the direction of either House of Parliament, nor are we to presume that he has any other sway in this House, but that which proceeds either from the solidity and strengths of his arguments, or from his superior art of persuasion: for which reason he can never be made to answer for any resolution of Parliament, or for anything that is done pursuant to the advice of Parliament. In all cases therefore he ought to be fond of having the advice or at least the approbation, of an independent and free Parliament; but more particularly in a case such as the present, where the most prudent councils may not be always attended with the wished-for success. In such cases, I say, more particularly, he ought in common prudence to choose and desire, that his conduct should proceed from the advice and resolutions of Parliament; because, whatever may be the event, he cannot be made to answer even by those who judge of things only by the event, which is the case of the greatest part of mankind, in this as well as every other country.

ii. *The Duke of Argyle speaking in the House of Lords, 1 March, 1739*

Source: *Parliamentary History* x. pp. 1136–7

I remember, my Lords, a very good saying of a noble Lord, who once sat in this House, it was the late Lord Peterborough: when he was asked by a friend, one day, his opinion of a certain measure; says my Lord, in some surprise, 'This is the first time I ever heard of it,' 'Impossible,' says the other, 'Why you are a privy counsellor!' 'So I am,' replies his Lordship, 'and there is a cabinet counsellor coming up to us just now; if you ask the same question of him, he will perhaps hold his peace, and then you will think he is in the secret, but if he opens once his mouth about it, you will find he knows as little of it as I do.' My Lords, it is not being in the privy council, or in the cabinet council, one must be in the minister's council to know the true motives of our late proceedings.

iii. *The Duke of Richmond, the Master of the Horse, to the Duke of Newcastle, 28 November, 1742*

Source: *Add. MS.* 32,699 f. 539

... In the first place I am delighted to see things go so well in the House of Commons. Then as to the House of Lords I take for granted any attendance will be unnecessary. And as for Cabinet

Councils they are quite out of fashion, so that all the business I can possibly have in town, is waiting upon my Royal Master, which I ever was and ever shall be ready to do when there is any real duty that calls me... but I own I cannot help preferring foxhunting, being with my family, to what may be called fiddle-faddle waiting, so I could wish to be excused going up till after Christmas. ...

iv. *The Duke of Newcastle to Henry Pelham, 12 August, 1750*

Source: W. Coxe, *Memoirs of the Administration of the Rt. Hon. Henry Pelham* (1829) ii. p. 371

I remember particularly, about a month or six weeks ago, talking of our foreign affairs, I said, 'I only write upon the secret part of them to my brother, and my lord Chancellor [Hardwicke]; the others know nothing of the matter.' The King answered, 'No; they two are the only ministers; the others are for show.' I did not dwell upon it, but left it.

3. THE PRIME MINISTER

i. (*a*) *Speech by Samuel Sandys in the House of Commons on the motion for the removal of Sir Robert Walpole, 13 February, 1741*

Source: *Parliamentary History* xi. pp. 1232–3

... I know, Sir, it will be objected, that as every material step in the late conduct of our public affairs, either at home or abroad, has been authorized or approved of by Parliament, what I have said must be looked on as a general charge against his Majesty's counsels and our Parliaments, rather than as a personal charge against any one minister; but this upon a due consideration, becomes the most heavy, and the most evident charge against the minister I aim at. According to our constitution, we can have no sole and prime minister: we ought always to have several prime ministers or officers of state: every such officer has his own proper department; and no officer ought to meddle in the affairs belonging to the department of another. But it is publicly known, that this minister, having obtained a sole influence over all our public counsels, has not only assumed the sole direction of all our public affairs, but has got every officer of state removed, that would not follow his direction, even in the affairs belonging to his own proper department. By this means he hath monopolized all the favours of the crown, and engrossed the sole disposal of all places, pensions, titles and ribbons, as well as of all preferments, civil, military or ecclesiastical.

This, Sir, is of itself a most heinous offence against our constitution: but he has greatly aggravated the heinousness of his crime; for having thus monopolized all the favours of the Crown, he has made a blind submission to his direction at elections and in Parliament, the only ground to hope for any honours or preferments, and the only tenure by which any gentleman could preserve what he had. This is so notoriously known, that it can stand in need of no proof. Have not many deserving gentlemen been disappointed in the preferment they had a just title to, upon the bare suspicion of not being blindly devoted to his personal interest? Have not some persons of the highest rank and most illustrious characters been displaced, for no other reason than because they disdained to sacrifice their honour and conscience to his direction in Parliament? ... Nay, has not this minister himself not only confessed it, but boasted of it? Has he not said, and in this House too, that he would be a pitiful fellow of a minister who did not displace any officer that opposed his measures in Parliament? ...

(b) *Sir Robert Walpole's denial of the charge, 13 February, 1741*
   Source: *Parliamentary History* xi. p. 1296

... But while I unequivocally deny that I am sole and Prime Minister, and that to my influence and direction all the measures of government must be attributed, yet will I not shrink from the responsibility which attaches to the post I have the honour to hold; and should, during the long period which I have sat upon this bench, any one step taken by government be proved to be either disgraceful or disadvantageous to the nation, I am ready to hold myself accountable.

To conclude, Sir, though I shall always be proud of the honour of any trust or confidence from his Majesty, yet I shall always be ready to remove from his counsels and presence, when he thinks fit; and therefore I should think myself very little concerned in the event of the present question, if it were not for the encroachment that will thereby be made upon the prerogatives of the Crown. But I must think, that an address to his Majesty to remove one of his servants, without so much as alleging any particular crime against him, is one of the greatest encroachments that was ever made upon the prerogatives of the Crown; and therefore, for the sake of my master, without any regard for my own, I hope all those that have a due regard for our constitution, and for the rights and prerogatives of the Crown, without which our constitution cannot be preserved, will be against this motion.

ii. *Lord Hervey stresses to George II in a letter dated 6 July, 1742, that he must have a minister who can ensure the support of the House of Commons*

Source: Lord Hervey, *Memoirs of the Reign of George II* (1848) ii. p. 586

It is as necessary, too, to the safe and quiet conduct of your Majesty's affairs that you should unite in the same person the favour of your closet and the power of it. At present, the favour is all bestowed on Lord Carteret, and all the power is exercised by Mr Pulteney. This cannot last; favour and power must go on together, or neither can go on long. It is as essential, therefore, towards constituting a minister who can subsist, to vest him with these two things, as it is to the fixing your Majesty's own power to reunite the authority of the Crown to the name of King.

iii. *The Duke of Newcastle to Lord Chancellor Hardwicke, 7 November, 1743*

Source: Add. MS. 35407 ff. 297–8

... My brother has been long taught to think by L-d Orford, that he is the only person fit to succeed him, and that he has a credit with the King upon that foot, and this leads him into L-d Orford's old method, of being the first person, upon all occasions. This is not mere form, for I do apprehend that my brother does think that his superior interest in the closet, and situation in the House of Commons, gives him great advantage over everybody else.

iv. (a) *The Duke of Newcastle to Lord Chancellor Hardwicke, 3 September, 1755*

Source: P. Yorke, *Life and Correspondence of the Earl of Hardwicke* (1913) ii. pp. 238–9

He [Pitt] then repeated, word for word, the same plan and system which Mr Legge proposed to me, the last year, viz:—that the business of the House of Commons could not go on without there was a minister (a subordinate one perhaps), which should go directly between the King and them; that if there was any objection to him he was far from desiring it himself, that any other person might be thought of; but that he could not, and would not, take an *active part* in the House of Commons without he had an *office of advice* as well as of *execution*, and that was the distinction he made throughout the whole conversation, that he would support the measures which he *himself* had advised, but would not, like a lawyer, talk from a *brief*.

(b) This excerpt is contained in Hardwicke's reply to the Duke dated 4 September, 1755.

Source: *ibid.* p. 245

If the King would give sufficient confidence and authority to his First Minister to confine it to this *subordinate* character, possibly there might be no great hurt in it; for I have long been convinced that, whoever your Grace shall make use of as your first man and man of confidence in the House of Commons, you will find it necessary, if he be a man of reputation and ability, accompanied with ambition naturally incident to such a character, I say, your Grace under these circumstances will find it necessary to invest him with more power, than from the beginning you thought fit to impart, either to Mr Legge or Sir Thomas Robinson.

v. *Source: ibid.* iii. p. 38

The precedents of my Lord Sunderland's and my Lord Godolphin's time have been over-ruled by the long habit of seeing Sir Robert Walpole and Mr Pelham in the House of Commons, which goes as far back as the memory of most people now [1757] sitting there, or indeed now in business, reaches.

vi. *Lord North to George III, 10 November, 1778*

   Source: J. Fortescue, *Correspondence of George III* (1928) iv. pp. 215–6

... That in critical times, it is necessary that there should be one directing minister, who should plan the whole of the operations of government, control all the other departments of administration so far as to make them co-operate zealously actively with his designs even tho' contrary to their own.

vii. *Lord North insisted on resigning when his Ministry lost support in the House of Commons, 18 March, 1782*

   Source: ibid. v. pp. 394–6

... When I had the honour of an audience with your Majesty this morning, I humbly endeavoured to state to your Majesty my reasons for thinking that the fate of the present ministry is absolutely and irrevocably decided. ... They [the Commons] are tired of the administration collectively taken, and wish at all events to see it alter'd...The torrent is too strong to be resisted; your Majesty is well apprized that, in this country, the prince on the throne, cannot, with prudence, oppose the deliberate resolution of the House of Commons; your royal predecessors (particularly King William the Third and his late Majesty) were obliged to yield to it much against their wish in more instances than one; they consented to changes in their ministry which they disapproved because they found it necessary to sacrifice their private wishes, and even their opinions to the preservation of public order, and the prevention of those terrible mischiefs, which are the natural consequence of the clashing of the two branches of the sovereign power in the state . . . The Parliament have altered their sentiments, and as their sentiments, whether just or erroneous, must ultimately prevail; your Majesty . . . can lose no honour if you yield at length, as some of the most renowned and most glorious of your predecessors have done, to the opinion of the House of Commons.

4. PARTIES

i. *Source:* Lord Hervey, *Memoirs of the Reign of George II* (1848) i. pp. 4–6

Whig and Tory had been the denominations by which men opposite in their political views had distinguished themselves for many years and through many reigns. Those who were called Whigs had been in power from the first accession of the Hanover Family to the Crown; but the original principles on which both these parties were said to act, altered so insensibly in the persons who bore the names, by the long prosperity of the one, and the adversity of the other, that those who called themselves Whigs arbitrarily gave the title of Tory to every one who opposed the measures of the administration, or whom they had a mind to make disagreeable at Court; whilst the Tories (with more justice) re-proached the Whigs with acting on those very principles and pushing those very points which, to ingratiate themselves with the people and to assume a popular character, they had at first set themselves up to explode and abuse.

The two chief characteristics of the Tories originally were the maintenance of the prerogative of the Crown and the dignity of the Church; both which they pretended were now become, if not by profession, at least by practice, much more the care of the Whigs. Nor were the Whigs quite innocent of this imputation; long service and favour had gradually taught them a much greater complaisance to the Crown than they had formerly paid to it, and the power of the Crown being an engine at present in their own hands, they were not very reluctant to keep up an authority they exercised, and support the prerogative which was their own present though precarious possession. The assistance likewise which the Whigs in power had received from the bench of bishops in parliamentary affairs, had made them show their gratitude in return, by supporting both them and the inferior clergy in all ecclesiastical concerns (except the suffering the Convocation to sit), with as much vigour and firmness as the most zealous of those who are called the Church Party could have done. The increase of the army and civil list, the repeated suspension of the Habeas Corpus Act, and frequent votes of credit in the late reign, were further instances that were often and not unreasonably given by the Tories of the Whigs deviating in their conduct from their original profession and principles.

Both Whigs and Tories were subdivided into two parties: the Tories into Jacobites and what were called Hanover Tories; the Whigs into patriots and courtiers, which was in plain English 'Whigs in place' and 'Whigs out of place'. The Jacobite party was fallen so low, from the indolence of some, the defection of others, and the despair of all, that in reality it consisted only of a few veterans (and those very few) who were really Jacobites by principle, and some others who, educated in that calling, made it a point of honour not to quit the name, though their attachment to the person of the Pretender was not only weakened but, properly speaking, entirely dissolved—their consciences quiet about his title, and their reverence to his character, their compassion for his misfortunes, and their hopes of his success quite worn out.

That which kept this party still alive, and gave it that little weight it yet retained in the kingdom, was, that all those who were by private views piqued at the administration without being disaffected to the government joined the Jacobites in Parliament, and pushed the same points, though on different motives; these only designing to distress the ministers, and those catching at anything that might shake the establishment of the Hanover family, and tend to the subversion of the whole.

By these means men oftentimes seemed united in their public conduct who differed as much in their private wishes and views from one another as they did from those they opposed; and whilst they acted in concert together, both thought they were playing only their own game, and each looked upon the other as his dupe.

ii. Sir Roger Newdigate was MP for Middlesex 1741–7, and for Oxford University 1750–80.

Source: Newdigate MSS. No. B2539/4 [*c.* 1765] f. 2

Whether you consider the origin of the terms Whig and Tory or the magnificent idea of the Friends of Political Liberty, those distinctions no longer subsist. In the two last reigns the Tories fully washed out the stain of their former conduct and were in fact the firm disinterested opposers of corruption and tyranny, the champions and preservers of civil liberty and as such they were deservedly named the Country Interest. The Whigs forfeited for ever the glorious distinction which they had obtained at the revolution, became the corrupt abject tools of ministerial powers and forged those chains for the people which will severely gall them if ever there should be a failure of virtue on the throne. From hence they were distinguished by the name of the Court Interest. The principles which they professed to abhor in the Tories were those they themselves followed, for it is not the name of George or James, the House of Stuart or the Hanover succession that makes the difference—a criminal attachment to persons to the destruction of every defence, every due weight in the scale of the constitution, of the independence of Parliament, the purity of the election and the elected that deserves the contempt and abhorrence of every true Briton. There are now properly four distinctions of men. Those formerly called Whigs who have no real quarrel with either the principles or actions of the present Administration but that they have lost their places and therefore will move Heaven and Earth to regain them— 2. Those of the same denomination who continue in and wisely submit to the most equitable sentiments of their masters, act with great union along with those who have been for above 40 years proscribed and banished from the royal presence, but who nevertheless have shewn all along that, though they hated the persons who ill treated them, they are well affected to the Protestant succession in the House of Hanover as the two last wars fully demonstrated. In that of 45 they associated for its support all over the kingdom whilst the W-es, H-ks[1] and nominal Whigs flew in their great benefactor's face and abandoned him because he would have shook off their yoke, and in the last war in every part of the kingdom they took up arms, gave up their opulence and ease to do the meanest military offices and subjected themselves to be led to death itself if necessary by the King's General in defence and support of his government. [Here Newdigate does not reconsider the third group, the main body of the Country Party who had been the Tories in the two previous reigns, and whom he has earlier dealt with at length.] The 4th sort hardly merit the distinction being a small part of those called the Country Interest, consisting of such as would raise themselves into position of advantage or such as are disgusted with the partiality of the new excise, but in other matters think with their party.

What are the true distinctions now remaining? Very little or none in principle—the possession of power and lucrative posts is alone the object of contention. There are few Jacobites, few Republicans, but the present disappointed and baffled opposition will not scruple to turn to either rather than continue unplaced and unpensioned.

iii. Burke's view should be compared with that of Bolingbroke—see *Portraits and Documents: 17th Century* p. 135

Source: E. Burke, *Thoughts on the Causes of the Present Discontents. Political Tracts* (1770) p. 78

. . . Party is a body of men united for promoting by their joint endeavours the national interest upon some particular principle in which they are all agreed. For my part, I find it impossible to conceive, that any one believes in his own politics, or thinks them to be of any weight, who refuses to adopt the means of having them reduced into practice. It is the business of the speculative philosopher to mark the proper ends of government. It is the business of the politician, who is the philosopher in action, to find out proper means towards those ends, and to employ them with effect. Therefore every honourable connection will avow it is

[1] Walpoles and Hardwickes.

their first purpose, to pursue every just method to put the men who hold their opinions into such a condition as may enable them to carry their common plans into execution, with all the power and authority of the state. As this power is attached to certain situations, it is their duty to contend for these situations. Without a proscription of others, they are bound to give their own party the preference in all things; and by no means, for private considerations, to accept any offers of power in which the whole body is not included; nor to suffer themselves to be led or to be controlled, or to be over-balanced, in office or in council, by those who contradict the very fundamental principles on which their party is formed, and even those upon which every fair connection must stand. Such a generous contention for power, on such manly and honourable maxims, will easily be distinguished from the mean and interested struggle for place and emolument.

iv. *The Influence of the Crown*

   (*a*) *Source: ibid.* pp. 79–80, 99–100

It behoves the people of England to consider how the House of Commons, under the operation of those examples, must of necessity be constituted. On the side of the Court will be all honours, offices, emoluments; every sort of personal gratification to avarice or vanity; and, what is of more moment to most gentle-men, the means of growing, by innumerable petty services to individuals, into a spreading interest in their country. On the other hand, let us suppose a person unconnected with the Court, and in opposition to its system. For his own person, no office, or emolu-ment, or title; no promotion ecclesiastical, or civil, or military, or naval, for children, or brothers, or kindred. In vain an expiring interest in a borough calls for offices, or small livings, for the children of mayors, and aldermen, and capital burgesses. His Court rival has them all. He can do an infinite number of acts of generosity and kindness, and even of public spirit. He can procure an indemnity from quarters. He can procure advantages in trade. He can get pardons for offences. He can obtain a thousand favours, and avert a thousand evils. He may, while he betrays every valuable interest of the kingdom, be a benefactor, a patron, a father, a guardian angel to his borough. The unfortunate independent member has nothing to offer, but harsh refusal, or pitiful excuse or despondent representation of a hopeless interest. Except, from his private fortune, in which he may be equalled, perhaps exceeded, by his Court competitor, he has no way of showing any one good quality, or of making a single friend. In the House, he votes for ever in a dispirited minority. If he speaks, the doors are locked. A body of loquacious place-men go out to tell the world that all he aims at is to get into office. . . . The power of the people, within the laws, must shew itself sufficient to protect every representative in the animated performance of his duty, or that duty cannot be performed. The House of Commons can never be a control on other parts of government, unless they are controlled themselves by their constituents; and unless these constituents possess some right in the choice of that House, which is not in the power of that House to take away. If they suffer this power of arbitrary incapacitation to stand, they have utterly perverted every other power of the House of Commons. The late proceeding I will not say, is contrary to law; it must be so; for the power which is claimed cannot, by any possibility, be a legal power in any limited member of government. . . .

Our constitution stands on a nice equipoise, with steep precipices and deep waters upon all sides of it. In removing it from a dangerous leaning towards one side, there may be a risk of oversetting it on the other. Every project of a material change in government so complicated as ours, combined at the same time with external circumstances still more complicated, is a matter full of difficulties; in which a considerate man will not be too ready to decide; a prudent man too ready to undertake; or an honest man too ready to promise. . . .

Indeed, in the situation in which we stand, with an immense revenue an enormous debt, mighty establishments, government itself a great banker and a great merchant, I see no other way for the preservation of a decent attention to public interest in the representatives, but the interposition of the body of the people itself, whenever it shall appear, by some flagrant and notorious act, by some capital innovation, that these representatives are going to overleap the fences of the law, and to introduce an arbitrary power. This interposition is a most unpleasant remedy. But, if it be a legal remedy, it is intended on some occasion to be used; to be used then only, when it is evident that nothing else can hold the constitution to its true principles.

(b) *Source:* D. Hume, *Essays Moral, Political, and Literary* (1862) p. 25

... the interest of the body is here restrained by that of the individuals, and the House of Commons stretches not its power, because such an usurpation would be contrary to the interest of the majority of its members. The Crown has so many offices at its disposal, that, when assisted by the honest and disinterested part of the House, it will always command the resolutions of the whole, so far, at least, as to preserve the ancient constitution from danger. We may, therefore, give to this influence what name we please, we may call it by the invidious appellations of *corruption* and *dependence*; but some degree and some kind of it are inseparable from the very nature of the constitution, and necessary to the preservation of our mixed government.

5. OPPOSITION

i. *Henry Pelham to the Duke of Newcastle, 8 October, 1741*

Source: W. Coxe, *Memoirs of the Administration of the Rt. Hon. Henry Pelham* (1829) i. p. 25

You fancy if you go out, that it will be you only, and that you shall never join in any opposition, professedly, against those with whom you have acted for so many years; but believe me, dear brother, before this session is at an end, you will be as declared an opponent as Lord Carteret or Mr Pulteney. They profess what you really think, and when you are out, will tell you they mean the same things; act for a time in subservience to you, till by degrees, from the Spanish War, down to the attempts to support the Pragmatic Sanction, you will have agreed so long with them that it will be difficult for you to separate from them in other points.

ii. *Lord Chesterfield to Bubb Dodington, 8 September, 1741*

Source: W. Coxe, *Memoirs of the Life and Administration of Sir Robert Walpole* (1798) iii. p. 580

I entirely agree with you, that we ought to have some meetings to concert measures some time before the meeting of Parliament, but that I likewise know will not happen. I have been these seven years endeavouring to bring it about, and have not been able. Fox-hunting, gardening, planting, or indifference have always kept our people in the country, till the very day before the meeting of Parliament.

iii. (*a*) *The Duke of Newcastle seeks advice from Lord Hardwicke, 8 April, 1757*

Source: *Add.* MS. 32870 ff. 376–88,

I detest in general the thought of Opposition. I have detested and blamed it in *others*, and therefore shall most unwillingly come into it *myself*. But, on the other hand, if *we* support these men and measures . . . to the public it is the same as if we were parties to the administration. For without *us*, this administration at present cannot go on. . . . Might not there be a middle way . . . might we not . . . act according to events, and as particular questions arise? This I know will be difficult and possibly in no shape satisfactory to our friends, who from thence may go part to one side and part to the other.

(*b*) *Hardwicke expresses forcefully his distaste for a formal opposition, 9 April, 1757*

Source: *ibid.* ff. 395–400,

For my own part, I am determin'd not to go into a *form'd general opposition.* I have seen so much of them that I am convinced they are the most wicked combinations, that men can enter into; worse and more corrupt than any administration, that I ever yet saw, and so they have appear'd in the conclusion. Therefore I see no other way at present, but to keep off from any absolute engagement with either party . . . and to oppose wrong measures, and concur in right ones, as particular questions shall arise, or be foreseen. I am sensible that this is not the political way to keep a party together, but that is not an objection against doing what I think in my own conscience to be right.

(c) Lord Mansfield, writing to Newcastle, endorses Hardwicke's view, 15 April, 1757

Source: ibid. ff. 427–31,

To mix in factious opposition, after so many years of honourable service, would blast your fame and reputation for ever. Specious pretences are never wanting; but in the present distress, it is impossible for any Court, how desperate soever, to make unconstitutional attempts; if they did, every man ought to oppose such attempts. But I speak of opposition to right or indifferent measures to force a change of hands. I desire for one to subscribe to Lord Hardwicke's declaration as the sentiment of a virtuous and loyal mind, to which I will inviolably adhere. I had much rather not exist than join at this time factiously in opposition to the King, whomsoever he employs. For his sake, for the sake of his successor, for the sake of government itself I would not do it.

(d) Newcastle conforms, 15 April, 1757

Source: ibid. f. 419,

I ... entirely agree with your Lordship not on any account *to enter into a formed General Opposition;* and I thought I had stated my objections to it in the strongest manner.

iv. Burke is referring here to the years immediately after the accession of George III.

Source: E. Burke, *Thoughts on the Causes of the Present Discontents. Political Tracts* (1770) p. 17

To the great Whig families it was extremely disagreeable, and seemed almost unnatural, to oppose the administration of a prince of the House of Brunswick. Day after day they hesitated, and doubted, and lingered, expecting that other counsels would take place; and were slow to be persuaded, that all which had been done by the cabal was the effect not of humour, but of system.

Relations between Hanoverian kings and their heirs apparent were notoriously bad; in consequence the Prince of Wales tended to become a focal point for opposition, especially among politicians who were out of office and who hoped to win preferment in the new reign.

i. *Source:* Lord Hervey, *Memoirs of the Reign of George II* (1848) ii. pp. 52–4

In short, at this time the Prince, who was not upon a foot of being spoken to by his father, was the only person who did not taste of his ill humour, and, though he was most of all in his displeasure, he least of all felt the effects of it. As the King hated, too, to talk of him almost as much as to talk to him, and disliked to have him the subject of his conversation almost as much as he did to have him the object of his sight, so he was as little apt to rail at him directly when he was absent as to snub him when he was present; though by a side-wind sometimes he took the pleasure of laying it on him pretty thick.

[The King said] 'One very often sees fathers and sons very little alike; a wise father has very often a fool for his son. One sees a father a very brave man, and his son a scoundrel; a father very honest, and his son a knave; a father a man of truth, and his son a great liar; in short, a father that has all sorts of good qualities, and a son that is good for nothing. But his Majesty drew this picture of a father and a son with so much eagerness, complimenting the one so strongly, and inveighing against the other so vehemently, that the Queen (though a good deal mistress of her countenance), looking towards Lord Hervey, betrayed that she took the parallel as it was meant; and the King himself, feeling he had pushed it too far, turned off the ridicule he thought he had incurred with quickness enough, by saying that sometimes it was just the reverse, and that very disagreeable fathers had very agreeable men for their sons. I suppose in this case he thought of his own father, as in the other he did of his own son.

One morning while he was dressing, before the company was

let in, and when nobody but those who had the privilege of the bedchamber were present, he indulged himself in another sally of this kind against his son, by saying, whilst he was talking of the actors that he had seen in the play of Harry the Fourth the night before, that there were some really very good ones, but for the Prince of Wales, he must own he never saw so awkward a fellow and so mean a looking scoundrel in his life. Everybody who was present, I believe, had the same thought, but all very properly pretended to understand his Majesty literally, joined in the censure, and abused the theatrical Prince of Wales for a quarter of an hour together.

ii. *Source: Marchmont Papers* (1831) i. p. 84

The Prince [of Wales], having closeted Lord Harrington to no purpose, had at last said to 'em, 'My Lord, remember the King is sixty-one, and I am thirty-seven.'

iii. *Hardwicke is here writing to Newcastle in 1757*

Source: P. Yorke, *Life and Correspondence of the Earl of Hardwicke* (1913) ii. p. 392

A scheme must be found which may, if possible, unite the whole royal family, and bring *the succession* to support and give quiet to *the possession.*

7. MEMBERSHIP OF PARLIAMENT

i. *The Peerage Bill, 1719*

Source: D. O. Dykes, *Source Book of Constitutional History from 1660* (1930) p. 185

... That the number of peers of Great Britain, on the part of England, shall not be enlarged, without precedent right, beyond six of what they are at present; but as any of the said present peers, or such six new peers, in case they be created, shall fail, their numbers may be supplied by new creations of commoners of Great Britain born within the kingdom of Great Britain or Ireland, or any of the dominions thereunto belonging, or born of British parents, and so, as often as failure shall happen.

ii. The View of Speaker Onslow

Onslow was Speaker of the House of Commons from 1728 to 1761.

Source: J. Hatsell, *Precedents of Proceedings in the House of Commons* (1796) ii. p. 71

Every member, as soon as he is chosen, becomes a representative of the whole body of the Commons, without any distinction of the place from whence he is sent to Parliament. Instructions, therefore, from particular constituents to their own members, are or can be only of information, advice, and recommendation (which they have an undoubted right to offer, if done decently; and which ought to be respectfully received, and well considered) but are not absolutely binding upon votes, and actings, and conscience, in Parliament. That every member is equally a representative of the whole (within which, by our particular constitution, is included a representative, not only of those who are electors, but of all the other subjects of the Crown of Great Britain at home, and in every part of the British empire, except the Peers of Great Britain) has, as I understand, been the constant notion and language of Parliament.

8. DURATION OF PARLIAMENT

The Septennial Act, 1716

Source: Statutes at Large v. p. 78

Whereas in and by an Act of Parliament made in the sixth year of the Reign of their late Majesties King William and Queen Mary (of ever Blessed Memory) intituled, An Act for the frequent meeting and calling of Parliaments: It was among other things enacted, That from henceforth no Parliament whatsoever, that should at any time then after be called, assembled or held, should have any continuance longer than for three years only at the farthest, to be accounted from the day on which by the Writ of Summons the said Parliament should be appointed to meet: and whereas it hath been found by experience, that the said clause hath proved very grievous and burthensome, by occasioning much greater and more continued expenses in order to Elections of Members to serve in Parliament, and more violent and lasting heats and animosities among the subjects of this realm, than were ever known before the said Clause was enacted; and the said Provision, if it should continue, may probably at this juncture, when a restless and Popish faction are designing and endeavouring to renew the rebellion within this kingdom, and an invasion from abroad, be destructive to the peace and security of the government; Be it enacted. . . . That this present Parliament, and all Parliaments that shall at any time hereafter be called, assembled or held, shall and may respectively have continuance for seven years, and no longer, to be accounted from the day on which by the Writ of Summons this present Parliament hath been, or any future Parliament shall be appointed to meet, unless this present, or any such Parliament hereafter to be summoned, shall be sooner dissolved by His Majesty, His Heirs or Successors.

9. ELECTIONS

i. *Rotten Boroughs*

(a) *Source:* D. Defoe, *A Tour Through the Whole Island of Great Britain* (1726) I. i. p. 62

Plate 21

. . . Here in the compass of about six miles are three borough towns, sending members to Parliament (viz.) Shoreham, Bramber, and Stenning: and Shoreham, Stenning are tolerable little market-towns; but Bramber (a little ruin of an old castle excepted) hardly deserves the name of a town, having not above fifteen or sixteen families in it, and of them not many above asking you an alms as you ride by; the chiefest house in the town is a tavern, and here, as I have been told, the vintner, or alehouse-keeper rather, for he hardly deserv'd the name of a vintner, boasted, that upon an election, just then over, he had made £300 of one pipe of canary.

This is the second town in this county, where the elections have been so scandalously mercenary; and of whom it is said, there was in one king's reign more money spent at elections, than all the lands in the parishes were worth, at twenty years purchase; the other town I mean is Winchelsea, a town, if it deserves the name of a town, where the ancient gates stand near three miles from one another over the fields, and where the ruins are so bury'd, that they have made good corn fields of the streets, and the plough goes over the foundations, nay, over the first floors of the houses, and where nothing of a town but the destruction of it seems to remain; yet at one election for this town the strife was such between Sir John Banks, father-in-law to the Earl of Aylesford, and Colonel Draper, a neighbouring gentleman, that I was told in the country the latter spent £11,000 at one election, and yet lost it too; what the other spent who opposed him, may be guessed at, seeing he that spent most was always sure to carry it in those days.

(b) *Source: ibid.* I. iii. p. 27

... Old Sarum is ... a double entrenchment, with a deep graffe, or ditch, to either of them; the area about 100 yards in diameter, taking in the whole crown of the hill, and thereby rendering the ascent very difficult. Near this, there is one farm house, which is all the remains I could see of any town in or near the place, for the encampment has no resemblance of a town; and yet this is call'd the borough of Old Sarum, and sends two members to Parliament; who, those members can justly say, they represent, would be hard for them to answer.

ii. *Buying a Seat*

Source: Le Blanc, *Letters on the English and French Nations* (1747) ii. pp. 89–91

... The point of most importance to this nation, is the election of the members to serve in the Lower House. The most virtuous, the wisest, the most zealous man ought here to be preferred: but he that is most prodigal, usually carries the day. The people formerly paid those whom they charged with the defence of their rights: now, they sell their votes to those who will give the highest price. Every man who is able to spend much is sure of making a party, but not of being elected: for if he has got a competitor who spends more, in all probability the latter will have the plurality of voices. Some get into Parliament to pay their debts; others run into debt to get into Parliament. Many ruin themselves in vain to obtain this honour. But often the candidates themselves do not pay this expense, but the heads of their party undertake to discharge it. . . .

During these times of election, the candidates or those who undertake to support them, are obliged to keep an open table, and sometimes they have three hundred persons to treat in a day. He who makes the most people drunk may depend upon the greatest number of votes. Good strong beer will effect all you want with the toping countryman; but they that are sober must be won over with money. The man of interest, who can bring in others, will have twenty, and sometimes thirty guineas for his own vote. He that will give the price may have all the votes he can desire . . . There are some gentlemen who carry this complaisance to the common people yet farther. At those shows which are so much in fashion among the English, and which furnish them with occasions of debauchery at least as much as of exercise, I mean the horse-races, I have seen very great lords drink bumper after bumper, to the health of the beggarly populace that surrounded them; I have seen them when the country fellows threw their hats up in the air, pull off their own periwigs and degrade not only their rank, but humanity itself, to please a vile mob. This is what they call making themselves popular. . . . Three months ago, I was coming to London with one of the members of Parliament, and we arrived at Leicester the same evening that there had been an election . . . the country party having carried their point. The streets, full on both sides with people who were both drunk and insolent, were also filled with brutal acclamations of joy. Everywhere were bon-fires at a small distance from each other; all the houses of the victorious party were illuminated, and the zeal of the master within was known by the number of candles in his windows. According to this rule of judging, the greatest enemy the ministry had in the town was a butcher. The streets being so very light, some of the people unluckily knew the arms of the coach. They told the mob, who crowded about us, and called us Whigs, and traitors to our country. We narrowly escaped being treated with blows instead of words, because they saw us drive into an inn which was not illuminated.

The night before there had been tumultuous assemblies of the populace, and seditious bills fixed up at all the gates, which imported nothing less than burning the houses, and cutting the throats of all the adverse party. Such is the drunkenness and confusion that usually attend these elections.

iii. *The Middlesex Election and its Sequel*
   Source: Commons' Journals xxxviii. p. 977

The House was moved, That the entry in the Journal of the House, of the 17th day of February 1769, of the resolution, 'That John Wilkes, Esquire, having been in this Session of Parliament expelled this House, was and is incapable of being elected a Member to serve in this present Parliament,' might be read.

And the same being read accordingly; A Motion was made, and the Question being put, That the said Resolution be expunged from the Journals of this House, as being subversive of the Rights of the whole Body of Electors of this Kingdom:—

The House divided.
The yeas went forth.

Tellers for the Yeas	{ Sir Philip Jennings Clerke Mr Byng }	115
Tellers for the Noes	{ Mr John St John Sir William Augustus Cunynghame }	47

So it was resolved in the affirmative.

And the same was expunged, by the Clerk, at the Table accordingly.

i. *Dunning's Motion, 1780*

    Source: *Parliamentary History* xxi. p. 340

'That it is necessary to declare, that the influence of the Crown has increased, is increasing, and ought to be diminished.'

... At 12 o'clock the Committee divided: For Mr Dunning's Motion 233. Against it 215—Majority 18. ...

'That it is the opinion of this Committee, that it is competent to this House to examine into, and to correct abuses in the expenditure of the civil list revenues, as well as in every other branch of the public revenue, whenever it shall seem expedient to the wisdom of this House so to do. ...'

The question being called for, the motion was agreed to without a division.

ii. *Civil Establishment Act, 1782*

    (*a*) Source: *Statutes at Large* xxxiv. p. 143

An Act for enabling his Majesty to discharge the debt contracted upon his civil list revenues; and for preventing the same from being in arrear for the future, by regulating the mode of payments out of the said revenues, and by suppressing or regulating certain offices therein mentioned, which are now paid out of the revenues of the civil list.

Whereas his Majesty, from his paternal regard to the welfare of his faithful people, from his desire to discharge the debt on his civil list, without any new burthen to the public, for preventing the growth of a like debt for the future, as well as for introducing a better order and economy in the civil list establishments, and for the better security of the liberty and independency of Parliament, has been pleased to order, that the office commonly called or known by the name of *Third Secretary of State*, or *Secretary of State for the Colonies*; the office or establishment commonly known by the name and description of *The Board of Trade and Plantations*; the offices of lords of police in *Scotland;* the principal officers of the board of works; the principal officers of the great wardrobe; the principal officers of the jewel office; the treasurer of the chamber; the cofferer of the household; the officers of the six clerks of the board of green cloth; the office of paymaster of the pensions; the office of master of the harriers and fox hounds; and also the office of master of the stag hounds, should be suppressed: wherefore, for carrying his Majesty's said gracious order into execution ... be it enacted. ... That ... the office commonly known by the name of *Third Secretary of State,* or *Secretary of State for the Colonies* [etc.] ... and all and every of the offices aforesaid, together with certain of the offices dependent on or connected with the same, of which a list shall be entered in the exchequer ... are hereby utterly suppressed, abolished, and taken away ...

[The Act goes on to control expenditure of the revenues of the civil list, and to regulate the granting of pensions and salaries]

(*b*) *Source: Correspondence of Lord Auckland* (1861) i. p. 12

Burke's foolish bill has made it a very difficult task for any set of men to form or maintain an administration.

iii. *The Association Movement, 1780*

Source: C. Wyvill, *Political Papers* (1794) i. p. 426

At a Meeting of Deputies from the Counties of York, Surrey, Middlesex, Sussex, Gloucester, Hertford, Kent, Huntingdon, Dorset, Bucks, Chester, Devon, and Essex; from the Cities of London and Westminster, and Gloucester, and the Towns of Newcastle and Nottingham, holden at the St. Alban's Tavern, and afterwards by several adjournments at the Great-Room in King Street, St. James's, on Saturday the 11th, Tuesday the 14th, Wednesday the 15th, Friday the 17th, Saturday the 18th, and Monday the 20th days of March, 1780; the Rev. Christopher Wyvill, one of the Deputies from the county of York, in the chair.

... What is our situation at present? By the operation of a

despotic system, which has continued with very little intermission, near nineteen years, and is now almost completed by a dangerous administration, the very vitals of the constitution have received a mortal wound, not this or that partiality of the reigning mind has been gratified, but the whole capacity of popular freedom has been struck at. We are arrived at the crisis which the wisest of political writers have uniformly marked for the downfall of Britain, when the Legislative Body shall become as corrupt as the Executive and dependent upon it.

Let any man look back to the laws which have passed only in the ten last Sessions of Parliament, forming, as it were step by step, a code of prerogative, which has already brought within its vortex the primary part of civil, religious, commercial, and military administration, within the kingdom or its dependencies, not excepting from its vast control all the branches of the royal family, and but too probably the succession of the Crown. Let him look back to these, and then doubt if the Executive Power has not found its way to the corruption of the legislative. Let him behold a venal majority in the House of Commons, session after session, moving obsequious to the nod of the minister, and giving the Legislative sanction to propositions, not only big with the fate of their country, but often militating against the first principles of the constitution, and the declared voice of their constituents; while every effort of reason and argument, urged by an independent few, has only been answered by numbers, dumb to every other reply: and then let him judge how enormous that corruption must be. But let him bring his observation to the immense patronage of the Crown, diffused over this Legislative Body in the bestowal of offices, and where offices are too few, or not lucrative enough to satiate the corruption of individuals, in ruinous contracts, in profuse pensions, some known, and others studiously concealed: let these be considered, and the terms above-mentioned, in which the crisis of British freedom is marked, are indisputably fulfilled, the Legislative Body is as corrupt as the Executive and dependent upon it. . . .

Wherefore we do most anxiously recommend it to all classes of citizens, and especially to those who have votes for the returning of any members to Parliament, as they value their liberties, the preservation of their remaining properties, and the rescuing of their posterity from unconstitutional dominion, to unite themselves in a firm purpose of obtaining from their representatives those salutary reforms, (the outlines of which are hereafter submitted) by the establishment whereof, the door must be effectually shut on that corruption, and jointly and severally to persevere, regardless of every consideration to the contrary, until they shall have obtained the same. . . .

Resolved,

1st, That a diligent examination be made into all the branches of the receipt, expenditure, and mode of keeping and passing accounts of public money, in order to obtain the Plan of Reform requested by the Petitions of the People.

Resolved,

2nd, That there be sent to the House of Commons, in addition to the present representatives of counties, a number of members not less than one hundred; to be chosen in due proportion by the several counties of the kingdom of Great Britain.

Resolved,

3rd, That the members of the House of Commons be annually elected to serve in Parliament.

iv. *Pitt's Resolutions in favour of Parliamentary Reform, 1783*

Pitt's modest proposals were defeated, and he never again risked his majority in the cause of parliamentary reform.

Source: Parliamentary History xxiii. p. 829

. . . He [Pitt] then read his three resolutions, which in substance, were as follows: '1. That it was the opinion of the House, that the most effectual and practicable measures ought to be taken for the better prevention both of bribery and expense in the election of members to serve in Parliament. 2. That, for the future, when the majority of voters for any borough should be convicted of gross and notorious corruption, before a select committee of that House, appointed to try the merits of any election, such borough should be disfranchised, and the minority of voters, not so convicted, should be entitled to vote for the county in which such borough should be situated. 3. That an addition of knights of the shire, and of representatives of the metropolis, should be added to the state of the representatives.'

II. LIBERTY OF THE SUBJECT

i. *John Wilkes and No. 45 of the* North Briton, *1763*
   Source: *The North Briton* (1766) pp. 262–5, 268

The King's Speech has always been considered by the legislature, and by the public at large, as the Speech of the Minister. . . . This week has given the public the most abandoned instance of ministerial effrontery ever attempted to be imposed on mankind. The minister's speech of last Tuesday, is not to be paralleled in the annals of this country. I am in doubt whether the imposition is greater on the sovereign or on the nation. Every friend of his country must lament that a prince of so many great and amiable qualities, whom England truly reveres, can be brought to give the sanction of his sacred name to the most odious measures, and to the most unjustifiable public declarations, from a throne ever renowned for truth, honour and unsullied virtue. I am sure all foreigners, especially the King of Prussia, will hold the minister in contempt and abhorrence. He has made our sovereign declare, 'My expectations have been fully answered by the happy effects which the several allies of my Crown have derived from this salutary measure of the definitive Treaty. The powers at war with my good brother the King of Prussia have been induced to agree to such terms of accommodation as that great prince has approved; and the success which has attended my negotiation, has necessarily and immediately diffused the blessings of peace through every part of Europe.' The infamous fallacy of this whole sentence is apparent to all mankind: for it is known, that the King of Prussia did not barely approve, but absolutely dictated, as conqueror, every article of the terms of peace. No advantage of any kind has accrued to that magnanimous prince from our negotiation, but he was basely deserted by the Scottish Prime Minister of England.

He was known by every Court in Europe to be scarcely on better terms of friendship here, than at Vienna; and he was betrayed by us in the treaty of peace. What a strain of insolence, therefore, it is in a minister to lay claim to what he is conscious all his efforts tended to prevent, and meanly to arrogate to himself a share in the fame and glory of one of the greatest princes the world has ever seen? The King of Prussia, however, has gloriously kept all his former conquests, and stipulated security for all his allies, except for the Elector of Hanover. I know in what light this great prince is considered in Europe, and in what manner he has been treated here; among other reasons, perhaps, from some contemptuous expressions he may have used of the Scot: expressions which are every day echoed by the whole body of Englishmen through the southern part of this island.

The Preliminary Articles of Peace were such as have drawn the contempt of mankind on our wretched negotiators. All our most valuable conquests were agreed to be restored, and the East India Company would have been infallibly ruined by a single article of this fallacious and baneful negotiation. No hireling of the minister has been hardy enough to dispute this; yet the minister himself has made our sovereign declare the satisfaction which he felt at the approaching re-establishment of peace upon conditions so honourable to his Crown, and so beneficial to his people. As to the entire approbation of Parliament, which is so vainly boasted of, the world knows how that was obtained. The large debt on the Civil List, already above half a year in arrear, shows pretty clearly the transactions of the winter. It is, however, remarkable that the minister's speech dwells on the entire approbation given by Parliament to the Preliminary Articles which, I will venture to say, he must by this time be ashamed of; for he has been brought to confess the total want of that knowledge, accuracy and precision, by which such immense advantages both of trade and territory were sacrificed to our inveterate enemies. These gross blunders are, indeed, in some measure set right by the Definitive Treaty; yet, the most important articles, relative to cessions, commerce and the fishery, remain as they were, with respect to the French. The proud and feeble Spaniard too does not renounce, but only desists from all pretensions, which he may have formed, to the right of fishing—

where? Only about the island of Newfoundland—till a favourable opportunity arises of insisting on it there, as well as elsewhere. . . .

The Stuart line has ever been intoxicated with the slavish doctrines of the absolute, independent, unlimited power of the Crown. Some of that line were so weakly advised, as to endeavour to reduce them into practice: but the English nation was too spirited to suffer the least encroachment on the ancient liberties of this kingdom. 'The King of England is only the first magistrate of this country; but is invested by law with the whole executive power. He is, however, responsible to his people for the due execution of the royal functions, in the choice of ministers, etc., equally with the meanest of his subjects in his particular duty.' The personal character of our present amiable sovereign makes us easy and happy that so great a power is lodged in such hands; but the favourite has given too just cause for him to escape the general odium. The prerogative of the Crown is to exert the constitutional powers entrusted to it in a way, not of blind favour and partiality, but of wisdom and judgment. This is the spirit of our constitution. The people too have their prerogative, and I hope the fine words of Dryden will be engraven on our hearts:

'Freedom is the English subject's Prerogative.'

ii. *The Illegality of General Warrants*
Source: State Trials xix. p. 1167

His lordship [the future Lord Camden] then went upon the warrant, which he declared was a point of the greatest consequence he had ever met with in his whole practice. The defendants claimed a right, under precedents, to force persons' houses, break open escrutores, seize their papers, etc. upon a general warrant, where no inventory is made of the things thus taken away, and where no offenders' names are specified in the warrant, and therefore a discretionary power given to messengers to search wherever their suspicions may chance to fall. If such a power is truly invested in a secretary of state, and he can delegate this power, it certainly may affect the person and property of every man in this kingdom, and is totally subversive of the liberty of the subject. And as for the precedents, will that be esteemed law in a secretary of state which is not law in any other magistrate of this kingdom? If they should be found to be legal, they are certainly of the most dangerous consequences; if not legal, must certainly aggravate damages. . . . I still continue of the same mind, that a jury have it in their power to give damages more than the injury received . . . it is my opinion the office precedents, which had been produced since the Revolution, are no justification of a practice in itself illegal, and contrary to the fundamental principles of the constitution; though its having been the constant practice of the office, might fairly be pleaded in mitigation of damages.

[The jury found a general verdict for the plaintiff, Wilkes, with £1,000 damages]

iii. *Somersett's Case, 1772*

James Somersett was a slave brought by his master as a servant from Jamaica to England. He escaped but was recaptured, whereupon a writ of Habeas Corpus was sued for his freedom. The extract is from Lord Mansfield's judgement.

Source: State Trials xx. p. 1

The only question before us is, whether the cause on the return [to a Habeas Corpus] is sufficient? If it is so, the negro must be remanded; if it is not so, he must be discharged. Accordingly the return states, that the slave departed and refused to serve; whereupon he was kept, to be sold abroad. So high an act of dominion must be recognized by the law of the country where it is used. The power of a master over his slave has been extremely different, in different countries. The state of slavery is of such a nature, that it is incapable of being introduced on any reasons, moral or political, but only by positive law, which preserves its force long after the reasons, occasion, and time itself from whence it was created, is erased from memory. It is so odious that nothing can be suffered to support it, but positive law. Whatever inconveniences, therefore, may follow from this decision, I cannot say this case is allowed or approved by the law of England; and therefore the black must be discharged.

iv. *The Riot Act, 1715*

Source: *Statutes at Large* v. p. 8

I. Whereas of late many rebellious riots and tumults have been in divers parts of this kingdom, to the disturbance of the public peace, and the endangering of his Majesty's person and government. ... Therefore for the preventing and suppressing of such riots and tumults, and for the more speedy and effectual punishing the offenders therein; Be it enacted. ... That if any persons to the number of twelve or more, being unlawfully, riotously, and tumultuously assembled together, to the disturbance of the public peace, at any time after the last day of July, in the Year of Our Lord One thousand seven hundred and fifteen, and being required or commanded by any one or more Justice or Justices of the Peace, or by the Sheriff of the County ... by Proclamation to be made in the King's name ... to disperse themselves and peaceably to depart to their habitations, or to their lawful business, shall ... unlawfully, riotously, and tumultuously remain or continue together by the space of one hour after such command . . . that then such continuing together . . . shall be adjudged Felony without benefit of Clergy, and the offenders herein shall be adjudged Felons, and shall suffer Death. . . .

II. And be it further enacted. ... That the order and form of the Proclamations that shall be made by the authority of this Act, shall be as hereafter followeth (that is to say) the Justice of the Peace, or other person authorized by this Act to make the said Proclamation, shall, among the said rioters or as near to them as he can safely come, with a loud voice command, and cause to be commanded silence to be, while Proclamation is making, and after that shall openly, and with loud voice make or cause to be made Proclamation in these words, or like in effect:

'Our Sovereign Lord the King chargeth and commandeth all persons, being assembled to disperse themselves, and peaceably to depart to their habitations, or to their lawful business, upon the pains contained in the Act made in the First Year of King George, for preventing tumults and riotous assemblies.

'God save the King.'

v. *The Gordon Riots, June 1780*

Source: C. M. Clode, *The Military Forces of the Crown* (1869) ii. pp. 635–7

The Secretary at War's Order to the Guards to assist the Civil Power at Lord George Gordon's riots.

War Office, 5th June, 1780

Sir,

One of His Majesty's Principal Secretaries of State having transmitted to me the information that numbers of people are assembled in the City of London in a tumultuous manner, and are actually committing great outrages there, and desiring that immediate orders may be given to the Commanding Officer at the Tower to afford the Civil Magistrate such assistance as he shall think proper to demand for restoring the public tranquillity, I do hereby signify to you His Majesty's pleasure that you hold yourself and the Troops under your command in readiness to assist the Civil Magistrate in case he shall require it, and that upon his requisition, and under his authority, you do order, from time to time, such of the said Troops as shall be thought necessary for the purpose before mentioned, to march to the place or places which the Civil Magistrate shall point out.

I am, Sir, etc.

C. JENKINSON

Officer Commanding the Foot Guards at the Tower

❖

George I's Dislike of England

Source: Lord Hervey, *Memoirs of the Reign of George II* (1848) ii. pp. 28–31

Whilst the late King lived, everybody imagined this prince loved England and hated Germany; but from the time of his first journey, after he was King, to Hanover, people began to find, if they had not been deceived in their former opinion, at least they would be so in their expectations; and that his thoughts, whatever they might have been, were no longer turned either with contempt or dislike to his Electoral dominions. But after this last journey Hanover had so completed the conquest of his affections, that there was nothing English ever commended in his presence that he did not always show, or pretend to show, was surpassed by something of the same kind in Germany. No English or even French cook could dress a dinner; no English confectioner set out a dessert; no English player could act; no English coachman could drive, or English jockey ride; nor were any English horses fit to be drove or fit to be ridden; no Englishman knew how to come into a room, nor any Englishwoman how to dress herself; nor were there any diversions in England, public or private; nor any man or woman in England whose conversation was to be borne—the one, as he said, talking of nothing but their dull politics, and the others of nothing but their ugly clothes. Whereas at Hanover all these things were in the utmost perfection: the men were patterns of politeness, bravery, and gallantry; the women of beauty, wit, and entertainment; his troops there were the bravest in the world, his counsellors the wisest, his manufacturers the most ingenious, his subjects the happiest; and at Hanover, in short, plenty reigned, magnificence resided, arts flourished, diversions abounded, riches flowed, and everything was in the utmost perfection that contributes to make a prince great or a people blessed. . . .

In truth he hated the English, looked upon them all as king-killers and republicans, grudged them their riches as well as their liberty, thought them all over-paid, and said to Lady Sundon one day as she was waiting at dinner, just after he returned from Germany, that he was forced to distribute his favours here very differently from the manner in which he bestowed them at Hanover; that there he rewarded people for doing their duty and serving him well, but that here he was obliged to enrich people for being rascals, and buy them not to cut his throat.

❖

Walpole's Influence through Queen Caroline

i. Walpole's pride in his policy of 'Peace at any price' is here clearly seen.

Source: Lord Hervey, *Memoirs of the Reign of George II* (1848) i. pp. 396–8

All this summer the Queen used to see Sir Robert Walpole every Monday evening regularly, and at other times casually. . . . And what is very surprising, yet what I know to be true, the arguments of Sir Robert Walpole, conveyed through the Queen to the King, so wrought upon him, that they quite changed the colour of his Majesty's sentiments, though they did not tinge the channel through which they flowed. When Lord Hervey told Sir Robert he had made this observation, Sir Robert said it was true, and agreed with him how extraordinary it was that she should be either able or willing to repeat what he said with energy and force sufficient to convince another without being convinced herself. However, said Sir Robert Walpole, 'I shall carry my point at last; but you, my Lord, are enough acquainted with this Court to know that nothing can be done in it but by degrees; should I tell either the King or the Queen what I propose to bring them to six months hence, I could never succeed. Step by step I can carry them perhaps the road I wish; but if I ever show them at a distance to what end that road leads, they stop short, and all my designs are always defeated. For example, if we cannot make peace, and yet I can keep this nation out of war a year longer, I know it is impossible but England must give law to all Europe: yet this I dare not say, since even this consideration would not keep them quiet if they thought peace could not be obtained; and for that reason I graft as yet all my arguments on the supposition that peace will be effected. I told the Queen this morning, "Madam, that there are fifty thousand men slain this year in Europe, and not one Englishman; and besides the satisfaction it is to one's good nature to make this reflection, considering they owe their safety and their lives to those under whose care and protection they are . . . it is no immaterial circumstance to be able to say, that, whilst all the rest of Europe has paid their share to this diminution of their common strength, England remains in its full and unimpaired vigour." '

ii. *Source: ibid.* i. pp. 416–7

Sir Robert thanked her extremely for all her goodness and kind thoughts of him: 'You know, Madam (said he), I can do nothing without you; whatever my industry and watchfulness for your interest and welfare suggest, it is you must execute: you, Madam, are the sole mover of this Court; whenever your hand stops, every-thing must stand still, and, whenever that spring is changed, the whole system and every inferior wheel must be changed too. If I can boast of any success in carrying on the King's affairs, it is a success, I am very free to own, I never could have had but by the mediation of your Majesty.'

iii. *Source: ibid.* ii. pp. 523–4

'Oh! my Lord,' said Sir Robert, 'if this woman should die, what a scene of confusion will be here! Who can tell into what hands the King will fall? Or who will have the management of him? I defy the ablest person in this kingdom to foresee what will be the consequence of the great event.' 'For my own part,' replied Lord Hervey, 'I have not the least doubt how it will be. He will cry for her for a fortnight, forget her in a month, have two or three women that he will pass his time with; but whilst they have most of his time, a little of his money, less of his confidence, and no power, you will have all the credit, more power than ever you had, and govern him more absolutely than ever you did. Your credit before was through the medium of the Queen, and all power through a medium must be weaker than when it operates directly. Besides, Sir, all princes must now and then be deceived by their ministers, and as the King is much easier deceived than the Queen so your task, whenever that task is deceiving, will be much less difficult than it was before. In the first place, because the King is naturally much less suspicious than the Queen; in the next, because he is less penetrating; and lastly, because he cares much less to converse with different people, and will hear nobody talk to him of business but yourself.'

❖

The Jacobite Rebellions

i. *1715. The lack of leadership of the Old Pretender*

This was one of the chief reasons for the failure of the Rebellion.

Source: A true Account of the Proceedings at Perth, Written by a Rebel (1716) p. 20

I must not conceal that when we saw the man whom they called our King, we found ourselves not at all animated by his presence, and if he was disappointed in us, we were tenfold more so in him. We saw nothing in him that looked like spirit. He never appeared with cheerfulness and vigour to animate us. His countenance looked extremely heavy. He cared not to come abroad among us soldiers, or to see us handle our arms or do our exercises. Some said, the circumstances he found us in dejected him; I am sure the figure he made dejected us; and had he sent us but 3,000 men of good hopes, and never himself come among us, we had done other things than we have now.

ii. *1745. Treatment of prisoners after Culloden*

Source: D. G. Forbes, Jacobite Memoirs (1815) ii. pp. 232–3

It is a fact undeniable, and known to almost everybody, that upon Friday the 18th of April, which was the second day after the battle, a party was regularly detached to put to death all the wounded men that were found in and about the field of battle. That such men were accordingly put to death is also undeniable, for it is declared by creditable people, who were eye-witnesses to that most miserable and bloody scene. I myself was told by William Ross, who was then

I GEORGE I

Studio of Sir Godfrey Kneller

2 (a) GEORGE II
Studio of Charles Jervas

2 (b) QUEEN CAROLINE
Studio of Charles Jervas

3 SIR ROBERT WALPOLE
Sir Godfrey Kneller

4 (a) WILLIAM PULTENEY,
EARL OF BATH
Sir Godfrey Kneller

4 (b) JOHN CARTERET,
EARL GRANVILLE
William Hoare

5 (a) HENRY PELHAM
after William Hoare

5 (b) THOMAS
PELHAM-HOLLES,
DUKE OF NEWCASTLE
William Hoare

6 (a) WILLIAM PITT,
EARL OF CHATHAM
Studio of Richard
Brompton

6 (b) HENRY FOX,
LORD HOLLAND
after Sir Joshua Reynolds

7 (a) GEORGE III
Studio of Allan Ramsay

7 (b) JOHN STUART,
EARL OF BUTE
after Allan Ramsay

8 (a) CHARLES
WATSON-WENTWORTH,
MARQUIS OF ROCKINGHAM
after Sir Joshua Reynolds

8 (b) FREDERICK, LORD
NORTH
Nathaniel Dance

9 (a) EDMUND
BURKE

Copy after Sir
Joshua
Reynolds

9 (b) WILLIAM PETTY,
EARL OF SHELBURNE

after Gainsborough

10 (a) ROBERT,
LORD CLIVE
Nathaniel Dance

10 (b) WARREN HASTINGS
after Sir Joshua Reynolds

(a) JOHN WESLEY
Nathaniel Hone

11 (b) SAMUEL JOHNSON
Sir Joshua Reynolds

12 PRIOR PARK, BATH

13 (a)   ST JAMES STREET, LONDON, IN 1792

13 (b)   LANSDOWN CRESCENT, BATH

14. THE LIBRARY, THE GEORGIAN HOUSE, SIR'S GRASS [illegible]

(iii) Hepplewhite

(i) Chippendale

(ii) Sheraton

15 (b) GEORGIAN CHAIRS

15 (a) CHIMNEY PIECE, KEDLESTON HALL, DERBYSHIRE

Robert Adam

16 VAUXHALL GARDENS

17   A COFFEE HOUSE

18 CRICKET PLAYED AT THE GENTLEMEN'S CLUB,
WHITE CONDUIT HOUSE, ISLINGTON

19   COCKFIGHTING
William Hogarth

20 GIN LANE

William Hogarth

21 THE POLLING BOOTH
William Hogarth

22 (a)   THE PRESS GANG
Cartoon by Gillray, 1779

22 (b)   THE EAST INDIA COMPANY WHARF
Peter Monamy

23   A FIRST-RATE OFF DEPTFORD, PROBABLY 1757

J. Clevely

24. THE TAKING OF QUEBEC, 1759

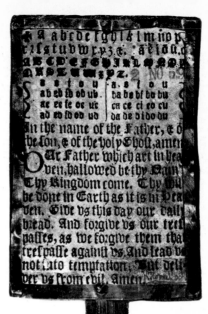

25 (a) A HORN BOOK

25 (b) JOSIAH WEDGWOOD'S ORIGINAL
PATTERN BOOK AND 3 PLATES

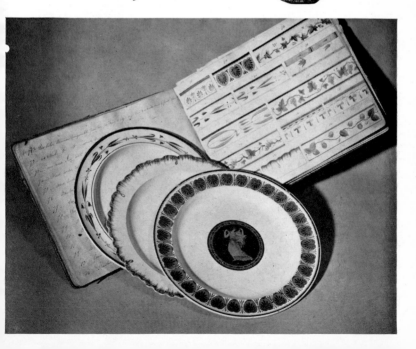

26 A COACH ON THE DOVER ROAD

27 A BROAD-WHEELED WAGGON

28 HYDE PARK TURNPIKE, 1792

29 THE BARTON AQUEDUCT, 1761

This four Wheel Drill Plow, with a Seed and a Manure Hopper, was first Invented in the Year 1745. and is now in Use with Wᵐ Ellis at Little Gaddesden near Hempstead in Herfordshire. where any person may view the same. It is so light that a Man may Draw it. but Generally drawn by a Pony or little Horse.

30 A SEED DRILL, 1745

Trowell & Ellis: *Farmer's Instructor*, 1750

(a) Sheep

(i) 1680

(ii) 1808

31 IMPROVEMENTS IN
BREEDING

(b) Cattle

32   ALL SAINTS CHURCH, WORCESTER

grieve[1] to my Lord President, that twelve wounded men were carried out of his house, and shot in a hollow, which is within very short distance of the place of action. . . . Orders were given, on the Friday, to an officer, Hobbie, or such a name, that he should go to the field of battle, and cause carry there all the wounded in the neighbouring houses, at a mile's distance, some more, some less, and kill them upon the field, which orders were obeyed accordingly. When these orders were given at the knee, an officer who was well pleased told it to his comrades; one of them replied, 'D-n him who had taken that order! He could not do an inhuman thing; though no mercy should be shewn to the rebels.'

❖

The South Sea Bubble, 1720

Source: The Case of the Borrowers on the South Sea Loans Stated (1721) pp. 6–7

The most prudent now began to blame themselves for the most unjust suspicions they had entertained of so good a project. A man of moderate fortune now seem'd poor by the vast riches all about him had so suddenly acquired. All grew impatient and uneasy, who were not in this stock, the managers were idolised, and only they were happy, who had directors for their friends. The merchant, who thro' a long diligence and great variety of hazard had gained a small Estate, grew mad to see so many idle fellows enrich themselves within a day or two. The honest country gentleman, who by good management and wise economy had been an age in paying off a mortgage, or saving a few small portions for his younger children, could not bear the big discourse and insults of this new race. Both laid aside their prudence, and at last became unhappy converts to South Sea; both were persuaded now to use their diligence, and recover that time their disbelief had lost them. The one despised his trade, and sold his effects, at any rate, to try his fortune: the

[1] Bailiff.

other mortgaged what he could, or sold it for a little stock or third subscription. And now both are undone, both beggars. I should think cases of such distress as these could not be reflected on without even humanity itself becoming painful; and yet, whether it proceeds from such cases being frequent and daily seen, or from an hardness of heart, which providence for a judgment has suffered to fall on us, I know not; but such cases are scarce pitied by us: every one still pursues his own interest, and seems to grudge the expense even of a few shillings, to save thousands from destruction.

The Excise Bill, 1733

Source: Lord Hervey, *Memoirs of the Reign of George II* (1848)
i. pp. 159–63, 175–6, 189

But this flame was no sooner extinguished in the nation than another was kindled, and one that was much more epidemical, and raged with much greater fury. Faction was never more busy on any occasion; terrors were never more industriously scattered, and clamour never more universally raised.

That which gave rise to these commotions was a project of Sir Robert Walpole's to ease the land-tax of one shilling in the pound, by turning the duty on tobacco and wine, then payable on importation, into inland duties; that is, changing the Customs on those two commodities into Excises; by which scheme, joined to the continuation of the salt-duty, he proposed to improve the public revenue £500,000 per annum, in order to supply the abatement of one shilling in the pound on land, which raises about that sum.

The landed men had long complained that they had ever since the Revolution borne the heat and burden of the day for the support of the Revolution government; and as the great pressure of the last war had chiefly lain on them (the land having for many years been taxed to four shillings in the pound), they now began to say, that since the public tranquillity both at home and abroad was firmly and universally established, if ease was not at this time thought of for them, it was a declaration from the government that they were never to expect any; and that two shillings in the pound on land was the least that they or their posterity, in the most profound peace and fullest tranquillity, were ever to hope to pay.

This having been the cry of the country gentlemen and landowners for some time, Sir Robert Walpole thought he could not do a more popular thing than to form a scheme by which the land-tax should be reduced to one shilling in the pound, and yet no new tax be substituted in the lieu thereof, no new duty laid on any commodity whatsoever, and the public revenue improved £500,000 per annum, merely by this alteration in the method of management.

The salt-duty, which had been revived the year before [1732], could raise only in three years what one shilling in the pound on land raised in one year; consequently, as that tax was an equivalent only to one-third of a shilling on land, if the remission of that shilling on land was further and annually continued, some other fund must be found to supply the other two-thirds.

This Excising of tobacco and wine was the equivalent projected by Sir Robert Walpole, but this scheme, instead of procuring him the popularity he thought it would, caused more clamour and made him, even whilst the project was only talked of and in embryo, more vilified and abused by the universal outcries of the people, than any one act of his whole administration.

The art, vigilance, and industry of his enemies had so contrived to represent this scheme to the people, and had so generally in every county and great town throughout all England prejudiced their minds against it; they had shown it in so formidable a shape and painted it in such hideous colours, that everybody talked of the scheme as a general Excise; they believed that food and raiment, and all the necessaries of life, were to be taxed; that armies of Excise officers were to come into any house and at any time they pleased; that our liberties were at an end, trade going to be ruined, Magna Carta overturned, all property destroyed, the Crown made absolute, and Parliaments themselves no longer necessary to be called.

This was the epidemic madness of the nation on this occasion; whilst most of the boroughs in England, and the City of London itself, sent formal instructions by way of memorials to their representatives, absolutely to oppose all new Excises and all extension of

Excise laws, if proposed in Parliament, though introduced or modelled in any manner whatsoever.

It is easy to imagine that this reception of a scheme by which Sir Robert Walpole proposed to ingratiate himself so much with the people, must give him great disquiet. Some of his friends, whose timidity passed afterwards for judgment, advised him to relinquish it, and said, though it was in itself so beneficial a scheme to the public, yet since the public did not see it in that light, that the best part he could take was to lay it aside.

Sir Robert Walpole thought, since he was so far embarked, that there was no listening to such advice without quitting the King's service, for as it was once known that he designed to execute this scheme, had he given it up, everything that had been said of its tendency would have been taken for granted. . . .

Sir Robert Walpole, therefore (who, if he could have foreseen the difficulties in which this scheme involved him, would certainly never have embarked in it at all), in this disagreeable dilemma chose what he thought the least dangerous path, and resolved, since he had undertaken it, to try to carry it through. His manner of reasoning was, that if he had given way to popular clamour on this occasion, it would be raised, right or wrong, on every future occasion to thwart and check any measure that could be taken by the government whilst he should have the direction of affairs, and that the consequence of that must be, his resignation of his employment or his dismissal from the King's service. . . .

At the same time many pamphlets were written and dispersed in the country, setting forth the dangerous consequences of extending the Excise Laws, and increasing the number of Excise-officers; showing the infringement of the one upon liberty, and the influence the other must necessarily give the Crown in elections. And so universally were these terrors scattered through the nation, and so artfully were they instilled into the minds of the people, that this project, which in reality was nothing more than a mutation of two taxes from Customs to Excises, with an addition of only one hundred and twenty-six officers in all England for the collection of it, was so represented to the whole country, and so understood by the multitude, that there was hardly a town in England, great or small, where nine parts in ten of the inhabitants did not believe that this project was to establish a general Excise, and that everything they ate or wore was to be taxed; that a colony of Excise-officers was to be settled in every village in the kingdom, and that they were to have a power to enter all houses at all hours; that every place and every person was to be liable to their search; and that such immense sums of money were to be raised by this project, that the Crown would no longer be under the necessity of calling Parliaments for annual grants to support the government, but be able to provide for itself, for the most part; and whenever it wanted any extraordinary supplies, that the Excise-officers, by their power, would be able at any time to choose just such a Parliament as the Crown should nominate and direct. . . .

This evening [9th April] Sir Robert Walpole saw the King in the Queen's apartment, just before the Drawing-room, and the final resolution was then taken to drop the Bill; but, as there was a petition to come from the City of London against it the next day, it was resolved that the Bill should not be dropped till that petition was rejected, lest it should be thought to be done by the weight and power of the City.

❖

The War of Jenkins' Ear, 1739

i. *Source:* Lord Hervey, *Memoirs of the Reign of George II* (1848) ii. pp. 484–5

Just before the King left Hampton Court a deputation of sixteen merchants came to him in great form with a petition signed by several hundred, to complain of the Spanish depredations in the West Indies, and beg his Majesty's protection and redress. The petition, which specified no particular facts, but was conceived in the strongest general terms, was referred to the Cabinet Council, and orders given by the King for a very strict examination to be made into the allegations of it. And the truth of the fact I believe was, that many of our merchants carrying on an illicit trade there, and being a sort of national smugglers, the Spaniards, irritated at this proceeding, had confounded the innocent with the guilty, and often seized ships they had no right to seize as well as those they had, and this way revenged themselves upon England for such illicit traders as had escaped them. Besides this, many of the Spanish governors in the West Indies, finding their account in conniving at this illicit trade in many instances by receiving money from the English merchants not to prevent it, the merchants were often secure in the ports where they ought to have been searched and stopped, and were all indiscriminately annoyed on the high seas, where the proper distinction was harder to be made. And the Court of Spain certainly acted unjustly to suffer this national havoc to be made by their *guarda costas*, instead of hanging their own governors for making this the only method of preventing this illicit trade from being carried on with impunity.

ii. *Source:* Samuel Boyse, *An Historical Review of the Transactions of Europe* (1747) i. p. 29

There was amongst the rest, one instance that made so much noise at this time, it cannot well be omitted. One Capt. Jenkins, Commander of a Scotch vessel, was in his passage home boarded by a *guarda costa*, the Captain of which was an Irishman. The Spaniards, after rummaging, finding their hopes disappointed, tearing off part of his ear, and bidding him carry it to the English King, and tell him they would serve him in the same manner if they had him in their power: this villainy was attended with other circumstances of cruelty too shocking to mention. The Captain, on his return, was examined at the Bar of the House of Commons; and being ask'd what his sentiments were, when threaten'd with death nobly reply'd, that he recommended his soul to God, and his cause to his country; which words, and the sight of his ear, made a visible impression on that great assembly.

❖

Anson's Circumnavigation

Source: George Anson, *A Voyage Round the World* (1748) pp. 192–203

But about ten o'clock at night, the ships being then within five leagues of the place [Paita in Peru], Lieutenant Brett, with the boats under his command, put off, and arrived at the mouth of the bay without being discovered, though no sooner had he entered it than some of the people on board a vessel riding at anchor there perceived him, who instantly getting into their boat, rowed towards the fort, shouting and crying, 'The English, the English dogs', etc., by which the whole town was suddenly alarmed, and our people soon observed several lights hurrying backwards and forwards in the fort, and other marks of the inhabitants being in great motion. Lieutenant Brett, on this, encouraged his men to pull briskly up, that they might give the enemy as little time as possible to prepare for their defence. However, before our boats could reach the shore, the people in the fort had got ready some of their cannon, and pointed them towards the landing-place; and though in the darkness of the night it might well be supposed that chance had a greater share than skill in their direction, yet the first shot passed extremely near one of the boats, whistling just over the heads of the crew. This made our people redouble their efforts, so that they had reached the shore and were in part disembarked by the time the second gun fired. As soon as our men landed, they were conducted by one of the Spanish pilots[1] to the entrance of a narrow street, not above fifty yards distant from the beach, where they were covered from the fire of the fort; and being formed in the best manner the shortness of the time would allow, they immediately marched for the parade, which was a large square at the end of this street, the fort being one side of the square, and the governor's house another. In this march (though performed with tolerable regularity) the shouts and clamours of threescore sailors, who had been confined so long on

[1] Prisoners captured in previous actions.

shipboard, and were now for the first time on shore in an enemy's country, joyous as they always are when they land, and animated besides in the present case with the hopes of an immense pillage— the huzzas, I say, of this spirited detachment, joined with the noise of their drums, and favoured by the night, had augmented their numbers, in the opinion of the enemy, to at least three hundred, by which persuasion the inhabitants were so greatly intimidated that they were much more solicitous about the means of flight than of resistance: so that though on entering the parade our people received a volley from the merchants who owned the treasure then in the town, and who, with a few others, had ranged themselves in a gallery that ran round the governor's house, yet that post was immediately abandoned upon the first fire made by our people, who were thereby left in quiet possession of the parade.

On this success Lieutenant Brett divided his men into two parties, ordering one of them to surround the governor's house, and, if possible, to secure the governor, whilst he himself at the head of the other marched to the fort, with an intent to force it. But, contrary to his expectation, he entered it without opposition; for the enemy, on his approach, abandoned it, and made their escape over the walls. By this means the whole place was mastered in less than a quarter of an hour's time from the first landing, and with no other loss than that of one man killed on the spot, and two wounded, one of which was the Spanish pilot of the *Teresa*, who received a slight bruise by a ball which grazed on his wrist. Indeed another of the company, the Honourable Mr Kepple, son to the Earl of Albemarle, had a very narrow escape; for having on a jockey cap, one side of the peak was shaved off close to his temple by a ball, which, however, did him no injury.

Lieutenant Brett, when he had thus far happily succeeded, placed a guard at the fort, and another at the governor's house, and appointed sentinels at all the avenues of the town, both to prevent any surprise from the enemy, and to secure the effects in the place from being embezzled. This being done, his next care was to seize on the custom-house, where the treasure lay, and to examine if any of the inhabitants remained in the town, that he might know what further precautions it was necessary to take; but he soon found that the numbers left behind were no ways formidable, for the greatest part of them (being in bed when the place was surprised) had run away with so much precipitation that they had not given themselves time to put on their clothes. In this general rout the governor was not the last to secure himself, for he fled betimes half naked, leaving his wife, a young lady of about seventeen years of age, to whom he had been married but three or four days, behind him, though she too was afterwards carried off in her shift by a couple of sentinels, just as the detachment ordered to invest the house arrived before it. This escape of the governor was an unpleasing circumstance, as Mr Anson had particularly recommended it to Lieutenant Brett to secure his person if possible, in hopes that by that means we might be able to treat for the ransom of the place; but it seems his alertness rendered the execution of these orders impracticable. The few inhabitants who remained were confined in one of the churches under a guard, except some stout negroes which were found in the town; these, instead of being shut up, were employed the remaining part of the night to assist in carrying the treasure from the custom-house and other places to the fort; however, there was care taken that they should be always attended by a file of musketeers.

The transporting the treasure from the custom-house to the fort was the principal occupation of Mr Brett's people after he had got possession of the place. But the sailors, while they wereithus busied, could not be prevented from entering the houses whch lay near them in search of private pillage: where the first things which occurred to them being the clothes that the Spaniards in their flight had left behind them, and which, according to the custom of the country, were most of them either embroidered or laced, our people eagerly seized these glittering habits, and put them on over their own dirty trousers and jackets, not forgetting at the same time, the tie or bag-wig and laced hat which were generally found with the clothes; and when this practice was once begun, there was no preventing the whole detachment from imitating it: but those who came latest into the fashion not finding men's clothes sufficient to equip themselves, were obliged to take up with women's gowns and petticoats, which . . . they made no scruple of putting on and blending with their own greasy dress. So that when a party of them thus ridiculously metamorphosed first appeared before Mr Brett, he was extremely surprised at the grotesque sight, and could not immediately be satisfied they were his own people. . . .

. . . The acquisition we made, though inconsiderable in comparison of what we destroyed, was yet far from despicable, for the wrought plate, dollars and other coin which fell into our hands, amounted to upwards of £30,000 sterling, besides several rings, bracelets, and jewels, whose intrinsic value we could not then determine; and over and above all this, the plunder which became the property of the immediate captors was very great, so that upon the whole it was by much the most important booty we met with upon that coast.

❖

The Seven Years' War

i. *The Battle of Minden, 1759*

From an account of the battle written by Lieutenant Hugh Montgomery, 9 August, 1759

Source: H. C. Wylly, *History of the King's Own Yorkshire Light Infantry* (1926) i. pp. 48–51

We marched from camp between 4 and 5 o'clock in the morning, about 7 drew up in a valley, from thence marched about three hundred yards, when an eighteen pound ball came gently rolling up to us. Now began the most disagreeable march that I ever had in my life, for we advanced more than a quarter of a mile through a most furious fire from a most infernal battery of eighteen-pounders, which was at first upon our front, but as we proceeded, bore upon our flank, and at last upon our rear. It might be imagined, that this cannonade would render the regiments incapable of bearing the shock of unhurt troops drawn up long before on ground of their own choosing, but firmness and resolution will surmount almost any difficulty. When we got within about 100 yards of the enemy, a large body of French cavalry galloped boldly down upon us; these our men by reserving their fire until they came within thirty yards, immediately ruined, but not without receiving some injury from them, for they rode down two companies on the right of our regiment, wounded three officers, took one of them prisoner with our artillery Lieutenant, and whipped off the tumbrells.[1] This cost them dear for it forced many of them into our rear, on whom the men faced about and five of them did not return. These visitants being thus dismissed, without giving us a moment's time to recover the unavoidable disorder, down came upon us like lightning the glory of France in the persons of the Gens d'Armes. These we almost immediately dispersed without receiving hardly any mischief from the harmless creatures. We now discovered a large body of infantry consisting of seventeen regiments moving down directly on our flank in column, a very ugly situation; but Stewart's Regiment and ours wheeled, and showed them a front, which is a thing not to be expected from troops already twice attacked, but this must be placed to the credit of General Waldgrave and his aide-de-camp. We engaged this corps for about ten minutes, killed them a good many, and as the song says, 'the rest then ran away'.

The next who made their appearance were some Regiments of the Grenadiers of France, as fine and terrible looking fellows as I ever saw. They stood us a tug, notwithstanding we beat them off to a distance, where they galled us much, they having rifled barrels, and our muskets would not reach them. To remedy this we advanced, they took the hint, and ran away. Now we were in hopes that we had done enough for one day's work, and that they would not disturb us more, but soon after a very large body of fresh infantry, the last resource of Contades, made the final attempt on us. With them we had a long but not very brisk engagement, at last made them retire almost out of reach, when the three English regiments of the rear line came up, and gave them one fire, which sent them off for good and all. But what is wonderful to tell, we ourselves after all this success at the very same time also retired, but indeed we did not then know that victory was ours. However we rallied, but all that could now be mustered was about 13 files private with our Colonel and four other officers one of which I was so fortunate to be. With this remnant we returned again to the charge, but to our unspeakable joy no opponents could be found. It is

[1] Two-wheeled covered carts carrying ammunition.

astonishing, that this victory was gained by six English regiments of foot, without their grenadiers, unsupported by cavalry or cannon, not even their own battalion guns, in the face of a dreadful battery so near as to tear them with grape-shot, against forty battalions and thirty-six squadrons, which is directly the quantity of the enemy which fell to their share. . . .

. . . The sufferings of our regiment will give you the best notion of the smartness of the action. We actually fought that day not more than 480 private and 27 officers, of the first 302 were killed and wounded, and of the latter 18. Three lieutenants were killed on the spot, the rest are only wounded, and all of them are in a good way except two. Of the officers who escaped there are only four who cannot show some marks of the enemy's good intentions, and as perhaps you may be desirous to know any little risks that I might have run, I will mention those of which I was sensible. At the beginning of the action I was almost knocked off my legs by my three right hand men, who were killed and drove against me by a cannon ball, the same ball also killed two men close to Ward, whose post was in the rear of my platoon, and in this place I will assure you that he behaved with the greatest bravery, which I suppose you will make known to his father and friends. Some time after I received from a spent ball just such a rap on my collar-bone as I have frequently from that once most dreadful weapon, your crooked-headed stick; it just swelled and grew red enough to convince the neighbours that I was not fibbing when I mentioned it. I got another of these also on one of my legs, which gave me about as much pain, as would a tap of Miss Mathews's fan. The last and greatest misfortune of all fell to the share of my poor old coat for a musket ball entered into the right skirt of it and made three holes. I had almost forgot to tell you that my spontoon[1] was shot through a little below my hand; this disabled it, but a French one now does duty in its room. The consequences of this affair are very great, we found by the papers, that the world began to give us up, and the French had swallowed us up in their imaginations. We have now pursued them above 100 miles. . . . They are now entrenching themselves at Cassel, and you may depend on it they will not show us their faces again during this campaign.

[1] A kind of halberd used by infantry officers.

ii. *The Taking of Quebec, 1759*

> Sources: i. W. W. Currie, *Life of James Currie* (1831) ii. p. 248
> ii. Dr James Graham, *History of North America* (1836) iv. p. 51
> iii. Captain John Knox, *An Historical Journal of the Campaigns in North America* (1769) ii. p. 70

Plate 24

i. General Wolfe kept his intention of attacking Quebec a most profound secret, not even disclosing it to the Second in Command, and the night before the attack nothing was known. The boats were ordered to drop down the St Lawrence.

ii. Silence was commanded under pain of death, which was indeed doubly menaced: and a death-like stillness was observed in every boat, except the one which conveyed the commander-in-chief, where, in accents barely audible to the profound attention of his listening officers, Wolfe repeated that noble effusion of solemn thought and poetic genius, Gray's *Elegy in a Country Churchyard*, which had been recently published in London, and of which a copy had been brought to him, by the last packet from England. When he had finished his recitation, he added in a tone still guardedly low, but earnest and emphatic, 'Now, gentlemen, I would rather be the author of that poem than take Quebec.'

iii. Our joy at this success is irrepressibly damped by the loss we sustained of one of the greatest heroes which this or any other age can boast of, General James Wolfe, who received his mortal wound, as he was exerting himself at the head of the grenadiers of Louisbourg ... After our late worthy General, of renowned memory, was carried off wounded, to the rear of the front line, he desired those who were about him to lay him down; being asked if he would have a surgeon, he replied, 'It is needless; it is all over with me.' One of them cried out, 'They run, see how they run.' 'Who runs?' demanded our hero, with great earnestness, like a person roused from sleep. The officer answered, 'The enemy, Sir; Egad, they give way everywhere.' Thereupon the General rejoined,

'Go one of you, my lads, to Colonel Burton; tell him to march Webb's regiment with all speed down to Charles's river, to cut off the retreat of the fugitives from the bridge.' Then, turning on his side, he added, 'Now, God be praised, I will die in peace': and thus expired. . . .

iii. *The Battle of Quiberon Bay, 1759*

This victory of Admiral Hawke, together with that of Admiral Boscawen over the Toulon fleet at Lagos, made the French invasion of England, planned by Choiseul, impossible. Hawke, forced to return to Torbay to refit his battered fleet, heard there that the Brest fleet, which he had been blockading, had escaped.

Source: Moorhouse, *Letters of English Seamen* (1810) pp. 119–22

Royal George, off Penris Point,
November 24th, 1759

Sir,

In my letter of the 17th by express, I desired you would acquaint their Lordships with my having received intelligence of eighteen sail of the line, and three frigates of the Brest squadron being discovered about twenty-four leagues to the north-west of Belleisle, steering to the eastward. All the prisoners, however, agree that on the day we chased them, their squadron consisted, according to the accompanying list, of four ships of eighty, six of seventy-four, three of seventy, eight of sixty-four, one frigate of thirty-six, one of thirty-four, and one of sixteen guns, with a small vessel to look out. They sailed from Brest the 14th instant, the same day I sailed from Torbay. Concluding that their first rendezvous would be Quiberon, the instant I received the intelligence I directed my course thither with a pressed sail. At first the wind blowing hard at S.b.E. and S. drove us considerably to the westward. But on the 18th and 19th though variable, it proved more favourable. In the meantime having been joined by the *Maidstone* and *Coventry* frigates, I directed their commanders to keep ahead of the squadron, one on the starboard, and the other on the larboard bow.

At half-past eight o'clock on the morning of the 20th, Belleisle, by our reckoning, bearing E.b.N. $\frac{1}{4}$N. about thirteen leagues, the

Maidstone made the signal for seeing a fleet. I immediately spread abroad the signal for the line abreast, in order to draw all the ships of the squadron up with me. I had before sent the *Magnanime* ahead to make the land. At three-quarters past nine she made the signal for seeing an enemy. Observing, on my discovering them, that they made off, I threw out the signal for the seven ships nearest them to chase, and draw into a line of battle ahead of me, and endeavour to stop them till the rest of the squadron should come up, who were also to form as they chased, that no time might be lost in the pursuit ... Monsieur Conflans kept going off under such sail as all his squadron could carry, and at the same time keep together; while we crowded after him with every sail our ships could bear. At half-past two p.m., the fire beginning ahead, I made the signal for engaging. We were then to the south-ward of Belleisle, and the French Admiral headmost, soon after led round the Cardinals, while his rear was in action. About four o'clock the *Formidable* struck, and a little after, the *Thésée* and *Superbe* were sunk. About five, the *Heros* struck, and came to an anchor, but it blowing hard, no boat could be sent to board her. Night was now come, and being on a part of the coast, among islands and shoals, of which we were totally ignorant, without a pilot, as was the greatest part of the squadron, and blowing hard on a lee shore, I made the signal to anchor, and come-to in fifteen-fathom water ... In the night we heard many guns of distress fired, but, blowing hard, want of knowledge of the coast, and whether they were fired by a friend or an enemy, prevented all means of relief. ...

As soon as it was broad daylight, in the morning of the 21st, I discovered seven or eight of the enemy's line-of-battle ships at anchor between Point Penris and the river Vilaine, on which I made the signal to weigh in order to work up and attack them. But it blowed so hard from the N.W. that instead of daring to cast the squadron loose, I was obliged to strike topgallant masts. Most of the ships appeared to be aground at low water. ...

In attacking a flying enemy, it was impossible in the space of a short winter's day that all our ships should be able to get into action, or all those of the enemy brought to it. The commanders and companies of such as did come up with the rear of the French on the 20th behaved with the greatest intrepidity, and gave the strongest proofs of a true British spirit. In the same manner I am satisfied would those have acquitted themselves whose bad-going ships, or the distance they were at in the morning, prevented from getting up.

Our loss by the enemy is not considerable. For in the ships which are now with me, I find only one lieutenant and fifty seamen and marines killed, and about two hundred and twenty wounded.

When I consider the season of the year, the hard gales on the day of action, a flying enemy, the shortness of the day, and the coast they were on, I can boldly affirm that all that could possibly be done has been done. As to the loss we have sustained, let it be placed to the account of the necessity I was under of running all risks to break this strong force of the enemy. Had we had but two hours more daylight, the whole had been totally destroyed or taken; for we were almost up with their van when night overtook us. . . .

I am, etc.,
Edward Hawke

iv. *The Year of Victories*, 1759

Source: H. Walpole, *Letters* (ed. P. Cunningham, 1857–9) iii. p. 258

To George Montagu Esq.

Strawberry Hill, October 21, 1759

Your pictures shall be sent as soon as any of us go to London, but I think that will not be till the Parliament meets. Can we easily leave the remains of such a year as this? It is still all gold. I have not dined or gone to bed by a fire till the day before yesterday. Instead of the glorious and ever-memorable year 1759, as the newspapers call it, I call it this ever-warm and victorious year. We have not had more conquest than fine weather: one would think we had plundered East and West Indies of sunshine. Our bells are worn threadbare with ringing for victories. I believe it will require ten votes of the House of Commons before people will believe it is the Duke of Newcastle that has done this, and not Mr Pitt. One thing is very fatiguing—all the world is made knights or generals. Adieu! I don't know a word of news less than the conquest of America. Adieu! yours ever.

P.S. You shall hear from me again if we take Mexico or China before Christmas.

v. *The Black Hole of Calcutta, 1756*

Source: A Complete History of the War in India, from the Year 1749 to the Taking of Pondicherry in 1761 pp. 18–21

[The Nabob of Bengal marched on Calcutta, which was abandoned by the commanding officer and the principal inhabitants] Mr Holwell, with a few gallant friends, and the remains of a feeble garrison, bravely defended the fort to the last extremity; but it was insufficient to protect an untenable place, or to affect an ungenerous enemy. The fort was taken on the twentieth day of June, 1756, and the whole garrison, consisting of 146 persons, being made prisoners, were thrust into a dungeon, called the Black-hole, from whence Mr Holwell, with twenty-one others, came out alive, to paint a scene of the most cruel distress, which perhaps human nature ever suffered or survived.

When he came to England, in the year 1757, he published, in a letter, an account of this shocking barbarity, in terms so pathetic and moving as cannot fail drawing pity from the most obdurate and savage breast. 'Figure to yourself,' says he, 'if possible, the situation of one hundred and forty-six wretches, exhausted by continual fatigue and action, thus crammed together, in a cube of eighteen feet, in a close sultry night in Bengal; shut up to the eastward and southward, the only quarters from whence air could come to us, by dead walls, and a door open only to the westward by two windows strongly barred within; from whence we could receive scarce any the least circulation of fresh air.

'Such was the residence of those unhappy victims for the space of twelve hours. When they had been in but a little while, a profuse sweat broke out on every individual; and this was attended with an insatiable thirst, which became the more intolerable as the body was drained of its moisture. In vain these miserable objects stripped themselves of their clothes, squatted down on their hams, and fanned the air with their hats, to produce a refreshing undulation. Many were unable to rise again from this posture, but falling down, were trod to death or suffocated. The dreadful symptom of thirst was now accompanied with a difficulty of respiration, and every individual gasped for breath. Their despair became outrageous. The cry of water! water! issued from every mouth; even the jemmadar [the serjeant of the Indian guard] was moved to compassion, at their distress. He ordered his soldiers to bring some skins of water, which served only to enrage their appetite and increase the general agitation. There was no other way of conveying it through the windows but by hats, and this was rendered ineffectual by the eagerness and transports of the wretched prisoners; who, at sight of it, struggled and raved even into fits of delirium. In consequence of these contests, very little reached those that stood nearest the windows; while the rest, at the farther end of the prison, were totally excluded from all relief, and continued calling on their friends for assistance, and conjuring them by all the tender ties of pity and affection. To those who were indulged it proved pernicious; for, instead of allaying their thirst, it enraged their impatience for more. The confusion became general and horrid, all was clamour and contest; those who were at a distance endeavoured to force their passage to the windows, and the weak were pressed down to the ground, never to rise again. The inhuman ruffians without derived entertainment from their misery; they supplied the prisoners with more water, and held up lights to the bars, that they might enjoy the inhuman pleasure of seeing them fight for the baneful indulgence. The miserable prisoners perceiving that water rather aggravated than relieved their distress, grew clamorous for air; they insulted the guard, in order to provoke them to fire upon them; and loaded the Suba [the Nabob of Bengal] with the most virulent reproach; from railing they had recourse to prayers, beseeching Heaven to put an end to their misery.

'They now began to drop on all hands, but a steam arose from the living and the dead as pungent and volatile as spirit of hartshorn; so that all who could not approach the window were suffocated. Mr Holwell, being weary of life, retired, as he had done once before, from the window, and went and stretched himself by the Reverend Mr Jervas Bellamy, who, together with his son, a lieutenant, lay dead in each other's embrace. In this situation he was soon deprived of sense, and lay, to all appearance, dead, till day broke, when his body was discovered and removed by his surviving friends to one of the windows, where the fresh air revived him, and he was restored to his sight and senses.'

vi. *The Battle of Plassey*, 1757

Source: J. Malcolm, *Life of Robert, Lord Clive* (1836) i. p. 263

I gave you an account of the taking of Chandernagore; the subject of this address is an event of much higher importance, no less than the entire overthrow of Nabob Suraj-u-Dowlah, and the placing of Meer Jaffier on the throne. I intimated, in my last, how dilatory Suraj-u-Dowlah appeared in fulfilling the articles of the treaty. This disposition not only continued but increased, and we discovered that he was designing our ruin, by a conjunction with the French.

About this time some of his principal officers made overtures to us for dethroning him. At the head of these was Meer Jaffier, then Bukhshee[1] to the army, a man as generally esteemed as the other was detested. As we had reason to believe this disaffection pretty general, we soon entered into engagements with Meer Jaffier to put the crown on his head. All necessary preparations being completed with the utmost secrecy, the army, consisting of about one thousand Europeans, and two thousand sepoys, with eight pieces of cannon, marched from Chandernagore on the 13th, and arrived on the 18th at Cutwa Fort, which was taken without opposition. The 22nd, in the evening, we crossed the river, and landing on the island, marched straight for Plassey Grove, where we arrived by one in the morning. At daybreak, we discovered the Nabob's army moving towards us, consisting, as we since found, of about fifteen thousand horse, and thirty-five thousand foot, with upwards of forty pieces of cannon. They approached apace and by six began to attack with a number of heavy cannon, supported by the whole army, and continued to play on us very briskly for several hours, during which our situation was of the utmost service to us, being lodged in

[1] Paymaster General.

a large grove, with good mud banks. To succeed in an attempt on their cannon was next to impossible, as they were planted in a manner round us, and at considerable distances from each other. We therefore remained quiet in our post, in expectation of a successful attack upon their camp at night. About noon the enemy drew off their artillery, and retired to their camp, being the same which Roy Dullub had left but a few days before, and which he had fortified with a good ditch and breastwork. We immediately sent a detachment, accompanied with two field-pieces, to take possession of a tank with high banks, which was advanced about three hundred yards above our grove, and from whence the enemy had considerably annoyed us with some cannon managed by Frenchmen. This motion brought them out a second time; but on finding them make no great effort to dislodge us, we proceeded to take possession of one or two more eminences lying very near an angle of their camp, from whence, and an adjacent eminence in their possession, they kept a smart fire of musketry upon us. They made several attempts to bring out their cannon, but our advanced field-pieces played so warmly and so well upon them, that they were always drove back. Their horse exposing themselves a good deal on this occasion, many of them were killed, and among the rest four or five officers of first distinction, by which the whole army being visibly dispirited and thrown into some confusion, we were encouraged to storm both the eminence and the angle of their camp, which were carried at the same instant, with little or no loss; though the latter was defended (exclusive of blacks) by forty French and two pieces of cannon; and the former by a large body of blacks both foot and horse. On this, a general rout ensued, and we pursued the enemy six miles, passing upwards of forty pieces of cannon they had abandoned, with an infinite number of hackaries,[1] and carriages filled with baggage of all kinds. Suraj-u-Dowlah escaped on a camel, and reaching Moorshedabad early next morning, despatched away what jewels and treasure he conveniently could, and he himself followed at midnight, with only two or three attendants.

It is computed there are killed of the enemy about five hundred. Our loss amounted to only twenty-two killed, and fifty wounded, and those chiefly blacks. . . .

[1] Two-wheeled bullock carts.

The next morning Meer Jaffier paid me a visit, and expressed much gratitude at the service done him, assuring me, in the most solemn manner, that he would faithfully perform his engagement to the English. He then proceeded to the city, which he reached some hours after Suraj-u-Dowlah left it.

◆

British Policy in India

i. *British Policy in India by Clive, 1759*

Source: J. Malcolm, *Life of Robert, Lord Clive* (1836) ii. pp. 119–23

Calcutta, 7th January, 1759

To the Rt. Hon. William Pitt, one of His Majesty's Principal Secretaries of State

Sir,

. . . The close attention you bestow on the affairs of the British nation in general, has induced me to trouble you with a few particulars relative to India, and to lay before you an account of the revenues of this country, the genuineness whereof you may depend on, as it has been faithfully extracted from the minister's books.

The great revolution that has been effected here by the success of the English arms, and the vast advantages gained to the Company by a treaty concluded in consequence thereof, has, I observe, in some measure, attracted the public attention; but much more may yet in time be done if the Company will exert themselves in the manner the importance of their present possessions and future prospects deserves. I have represented to them in the strongest terms the expediency of sending out and keeping up constantly such a force as will enable them to embrace the first opportunity of further aggrandising themselves, and I dare pronounce from a thorough knowledge of this country's government and of the genius of the people acquired by two years' application and experience that such an opportunity will soon offer. The reigning

Subah, whom the victory at Plassey invested with the sovereignty of these provinces, still it is true retains his attachment to us, and probably, while he has no other support, will continue to do so; but Mussulmans are so little influenced by gratitude that should he ever think it his interest to break with us, the obligations he owes us would prove no restraint . . . Moreover, he is advanced in years, and his son is so cruel, worthless a young fellow, and so apparently an enemy of the English, that it will be almost unsafe trusting him with the succession. So small a body as two thousand Europeans will secure us against any apprehensions from either the one or the other; and in case of their daring to be troublesome, enable the Company to take the sovereignty upon themselves.

There will be the less difficulty in bringing about such an event, as the natives themselves have no attachment whatever to particular princes; and as under the present government, they have no security for their lives and properties, they would rejoice in so happy an exchange as that of a mild for a despotic government; and there is little room to doubt our obtaining the Moghul's sunnud [or grant] in confirmation thereof, provided we agreed to pay him the stipulated allotment out of the revenues, viz., fifty lacs[1] annually. . . .

But so large a sovereignty may possibly be an object too extensive for a mercantile company; and it is to be feared they are not of themselves able, without the nation's assistance, to obtain so wide a dominion. I have, therefore, presumed Sir, to represent this matter to you and submit it to your consideration, whether the execution of a design, that may hereafter be still carried to greater length, be worthy of the government taking it into hand. I flatter myself I have made it pretty clear to you, that there will be little or no difficulty in obtaining the absolute possession of these rich kingdoms and that with the Moghul's own consent, on condition of paying him less than a fifth of the revenues thereof. Now I leave you to judge whether an income yearly of upwards of two millions sterling, with the possession of three provinces abounding in the most valuable production of nature and of art, be an object deserving the nation's attention, and whether it be worth the nation's while to take the proper measures to secure such an acquisition—an

[1] A lac is 100,000 rupees.

acquisition which, under the management of so able and disinterested a minister, would prove a source of immense wealth to the kingdom, and might in time be appropriated in part as a fund toward diminishing the heavy load of debt under which we at present labour. Add to these advantages the influence we shall thereby acquire over the several European nations engaged in the commerce here, which these could no longer carry on but through our indulgence, and under such limitations as we should think fit to prescribe. It is well worthy consideration, that this project may be brought about without draining the mother country as has been too much the case with our possessions in America. A small force from home will be sufficient, as we always make sure of any number we please of black troops, who being both much better paid and treated than by the country powers, will very readily enter into our service.

ii. *Pitt's India Act, 1784*

The effect of this Act was to establish a complicated dual system of government in India which remained until after the Indian Mutiny.

Source: Statutes at Large xiv. p. 477

. . . For the better government and security of the territorial possessions of this kingdom in the East Indies, be it enacted . . . That it shall and may be lawful to and for the King's Majesty, his heirs and successors, by any commission to be issued under the Great Seal of Great Britain, to nominate and appoint such persons, not exceeding six in number . . . being of his Majesty's most honourable privy council, of whom one of his Majesty's principal secretaries of state for the time being, and the Chancellor of the exchequer for the time being, shall be two, to be . . . commissioners for the affairs of India.

. . . and that the said commissioners shall have . . . the superintendence and control over all the British territorial possessions in the East Indies, and over the affairs of the united company of merchants trading thereto in manner hereinafter directed.

[The considerable powers remaining to the Court of Directors are detailed in the later clauses of the Act]

Burke made this speech during the impeachment of Warren Hastings.
Source: E. Burke, *Works* (1852) vii. pp. 26–8
Plate 22 (b)

The Company in India does not exist as a national colony. In effect and substance, nobody can go thither that does not go in its service. The English in India are nothing but a seminary for the succession of officers. They are a nation of placemen; they are a commonwealth without a people; they are a state made up wholly of magistrates. There is nothing to be in propriety called people, to watch, to inspect, to balance against the power of office. The power of office, so far as the English nation is concerned, is the sole power in the country. The consequence of which is, that being a kingdom of magistrates, what is commonly called the *esprit du corps* is strong in it. This spirit of the body predominates equally in all parts; by which the members must consider themselves as having a common interest, and that common interest separated both from that of the country which sent them out, and from that of the country in which they act. No control upon them exists; none, I mean, in persons who understand their language, who understand their manners, or can apply their conduct to the laws. Therefore, in a body so constituted confederacy is easy, and has been general. Your lordships are not to expect that that should happen in such a body which never happened in any body or corporation, that is, that they should in any instance be a proper check and control upon themselves. It is not in the nature of things. The fundamental principle of the whole of the East-India Company's system is monopoly in some sense or other. The same principle predominates in the service abroad and the service at home; and both systems are united into one, animated with the same spirit, that is, with the corporate spirit. . . .

By means of this peculiar circumstance it has not been difficult for Mr Hastings to embody abuse, and to put himself at the head of a regular system of corruption.

Another circumstance in that service is deserving of notice. Except in the highest parts of all, the emoluments of office do not in any degree correspond with the trust, nor the nature of the office with its name. In other official systems the style, in general, is above the function; here it is the reverse. Under the name of junior merchant, senior merchant, writer, and other petty appellations of the counting-house, you have magistrates of high dignity, you have administrators of revenues truly royal; you have judges civil, and in some respects criminal, who pass judgment upon the greatest properties of a great country. The legal public emoluments that belong to them are very often so inadequate to the real dignity of the character, that it is impossible, almost absolutely impossible, for the subordinate parts of it, which though subordinate are stations of power, to exist as Englishmen who look at a fortune to be enjoyed at home as their ultimate object, and to exist in a state of perfect incorruption in that service. . . .

Mr Hastings at the head of the service, with high legal emoluments, has fouled his hands and sullied his government with bribes. He has substituted oppression and tyranny in the place of legal government. With all that unbounded, licentious power which he has assumed over the public revenues, instead of endeavouring to find a series of gradual, progressive, honourable, and adequate rewards for the persons who serve the public in the subordinate but powerful situations, he has left them to prey upon the people without the smallest degree of control. In default of honest emolument, there is the unbounded license of power; and (as one of the honestest and ablest servants of the Company said to me in conversation) the civil service of the Company resembled the military service of the Mahrattas—a little pay, but unbounded license to plunder. I do not say that some of the salaries given in India would not sound well here; but when you consider the nature of the trusts, the dignity of the situation, whatever the name of them may be, the powers that are granted, the hopes that every man has of establishing himself at home—I repeat, it is a source of infinite grievance—of infinite abuse: of which source of corrupt power we charge Mr Hastings with having availed himself in filling up the void of direct pay, by finding out and countenancing every kind of oblique and unjust emolument; though it must be confessed that he is far from being solely guilty of this offence.

Another circumstance which distinguishes the East-India Company is the youth of the persons who are employed in the system of that service. The servants have almost universally been sent out to begin their progress and career in active occupation, and in the exercise of high authority, at that period of life which in all other places has been employed in the course of a rigid education. To put the matter in a few words, they are transferred from slippery youth to perilous independence, from perilous independence to inordinate expectations, from inordinate expectations to boundless power. School-boys without tutors, minors without guardians, the world is let loose upon them, with all its temptations; and they are let loose upon the world, with all the powers that despotism involves.

❖

The American War of Independence

I. WALPOLE ON COLONIAL TRADE, 1721-2

Source: W. Coxe, *Memoirs of the Life and Administration of Sir Robert Walpole* (1798) i. p. 163

In this situation of affairs, we should be extremely wanting to ourselves, if we neglected to improve the favourable opportunity which this general tranquillity gives us, of extending our commerce, upon which the riches and grandeur of this nation chiefly depend. It is very obvious, that nothing would more conduce to the obtaining so public a good, than to make the exportation of our own manufactures, and the importation of the commodities used in the manufacturing of them, as practicable and as easy as may be; by this means, the balance of trade may be preserved in our favour, our navigation increased, and greater numbers of our poor employed. I must therefore recommend it to you, gentlemen of the House of Commons, to consider how far the duties on these branches may be taken off, and replaced, without any violation of public faith, or laying any new burthen upon [the] people. And I promise myself, that by a due consideration of this matter, the produce of those duties, compared with the infinite advantages that will accrue to the kingdom by their being taken off, will be found to be inconsiderable, as to leave little room for any difficulties or objections.

The supplying ourselves with naval stores upon terms the most easy and least precarious, seems highly to deserve the care and attention of parliament. Our plantations in America naturally abound with most of the proper materials for this necessary and essential part of our trade and maritime strength; and if by due encouragement, we could be furnished from thence with those naval stores, which we are now obliged to purchase, and bring from foreign countries, it would not only greatly contribute to the riches, influence and power of this nation, but, by employing our own colonies in this useful and advantageous service, divert them from setting up, and carrying on manufactures which directly interfere with those of Great Britain.

2. THE MERCANTILIST OUTLOOK

A memorandum from William Shirley, Governor of Massachusetts, on the value of the colonies to England, *c.* 1750.

Source: Essex Record Office, Mildmay Archives (D/DM 01/41)

The principal articles, in which the value of these colonies consists, are

1. The addition of subjects which their inhabitants make to the Crown of Great Britain.

2. The consumption of British manufactures, and all other European commodities within them.

3. The fisheries carried on in the adjacent seas.

4. The several naval stores, with which they supply England.

5. The furs, tobacco, and rice, which are of the natural growth there.

6. The lumber and stores, with which they supply the English sugar islands.

7. The dominion and sovereignty of the Atlantic Ocean, which the possession of them must give the Crown that holds them.

As to the first article; the extent of the British Northern Colonies exclusive of Newfoundland, and measuring it upon the sea coast from Nova Scotia to Georgia, inclusive of both, is about five hundred leagues; and the depth of them goes as far back into the country as Mississippi and the South Sea. The eleven settlements, which are chiefly upon the sea coast, may be computed to contain about fourteen hundred thousand inhabitants, exclusive of Indian savages and negro slaves.

These inhabitants, within the compass of one hundred and forty years, from which time the utmost of the eldest of those colonies is to be dated, have, from small drafts made out of the Mother Country and her dependencies, chiefly in the beginning of their settlements, grown to their present number by the natural increase of the people, saving what addition they have received by such as have transplanted themselves from the northern parts of Germany; which may amount to about two hundred thousand in the colony of Pennsylvania.

It has been found from assessments made from time to time of the rateable polls within the province of the Massachusetts Bay, where there are now two hundred and forty thousand inhabitants, that, taking their increase at a medium from the first settlement of the colony to the year 1743, they have doubled their numbers once in every twenty years.

If this should not be thought an equal rule for estimating the future growth of the inhabitants within this province now, when their number is so large: yet it seems a moderate computation to reckon, that their present number may be doubled at the end of fifty years, and if that is a just rule for rating the natural increase of the inhabitants within the other colonies, as it seems to be, then the number of inhabitants within all the British Colonies in North America, may be expected, from their natural increase, and without making any allowance for the transplanting of Protestant families from the Palatinate, Swiss Cantons, and other Northern Parts of Germany, to amount at the end of that period, to about three millions.

The principal advantage accruing to the Mother Country, from the great number of inhabitants in her Northern Colonies, will appear from the consideration of what is mentioned in the second article, viz., the consumption they will occasion of British manufactures, as also of all other European commodities in general; which last must be landed and re-shipped in Great Britain (which is by the Acts of Trade, made Staple of them for all the English Colonies) before they can be imported into America. . . .

The third article is the fisheries carried on within the colonies. Very particular estimates have been made of the cod fishery, whereby the returns of it appear to be about one million sterling per annum. All this fish, except what is consumed in America, which is but an inconsiderable part of it, is exported to the Straits and Mediterranean, and there sold for gold or bills of exchange, payable in Great Britain, from whence returns are made to the colonies in English goods, so that the produce of this fishery as well as the profits of furnishing the outset of it, centre in the Mother Country. Besides this, a whale fishery is carried on within the province of Massachusetts Bay, from whence quantities of train oil are yearly exported to England; but as this holds, at present, no proportion with that of the cod fishery, and I can make no calculation of it, I do but mention it.

The profits of these fisheries are the more beneficial, as they are gained out of the sea (a fund not to be exhausted) and find employment for a number of hands, which might be useless, or of but small account on shore, as is found to be the case of most countries, with respect to the refuse part of the inhabitants; and fisheries are more particularly advantageous to a maritime state, as they breed up the best of sailors. The cod fishery, therefore, of New England has ever been justly esteemed a good nursery of seamen for the Royal Navy, and it has the advantage of the English colliery in this respect, that whereas five or six hands are sufficient to navigate a collier of large burthen, five times that number of hands is necessary to be employed on board a very small fishing vessel for navigating it, and in catching and curing the fish; all which may be reckoned good seamen, at least, very fit for immediate service on board the King's ships.

The article next to be considered is the naval stores. Every species of these is of the growth of the Northern Colonies. The Royal Navy is almost wholly supplied from the province of the Massachusetts Bay, and New Hampshire, with masts, yards, and bowsprits; as the shipping of England in general is with the pitch and tar from Carolina.

Upon this article it may be remarked, that it is an invaluable advantage to a maritime power to have its naval stores of the produce of its own dominions, independent of a foreign state, and not to be liable to be cut off from them by the accidents of war, or prohibition of the prince, in whose dominions they must be purchased; to have them likewise imported in its own shipping, at reasonable rates, and in exchange for its own manufactures.

The difference between being dependent on a foreign power for any of these stores, and having them of the growth of British territories, is remarkable in the article of tar. When Great Britain was obliged to take that species from the Northern Powers, the price of it rose to five pounds sterling a barrel, and either Sweden or Norway (I do not immediately recollect which) refused to let it be exported in English vessels. This imposition occasioned a bounty to be given by Parliament for the encouragement of making tar in the English colonies in North America; the effect of which has been to lower the price of it to a third part of what was before given; and to be paid for to subjects of Great Britain in English manufactures, instead of being paid for to foreigners in silver and gold.

It is next to be observed that the rich commodities of furs, tobacco, and rice are of the produce of the English Northern Colonies. There is likewise a fair prospect of Carolina's raising sufficient plantations of mulberry trees for the production of raw silk; its oranges are found to be near as good as those of Seville; and it is not doubted that the climate and soil of the British Northern Colonies is capable of producing a variety of wines that might vie with those of the growth of Europe.

The next thing to be remarked is, that the lumber, horses, and fish (not to mention the flour and pork), with which North America supplies the Sugar Colonies, are necessary for the carrying on the sugar works in the plantations there, and for the subsistence of their negroes; so that the support of those islands depends upon that of the English Northern Colonies; were these to be lost, the Sugar Islands would soon languish and decay to such a degree, as to be of very little value to the Mother Country.

The last advantage I shall specify, arising from the possession of the English Colonies in North America, is that the prince, which holds it, will be in a condition to keep the sovereignty of the Atlantic Ocean, through which the homeward-bound trade to Europe from the East and West Indies generally passes. This evidently appears from the consideration of the extent of the sea coast, which the colonies of North America take up, abounding with most commodious harbours, from whence the ships passing through those seas may be intercepted. France most sensibly felt the effects of it, during the late war in the captures made by the English of their trade in general returning from those parts; and it is well known that the harbour of Louisbourg is the rendezvous of the French East India and South Sea trade in their passage home to France.

It is evident, from what has been mentioned, how much the shipping trade, and maritime power, of Great Britain must be increased by the advantage arising to her from her colonies in North America; and, on the other hand, how much her power would be diminished, and that of France aggrandized if England should ever happen to lose them to France.

3. STAMP ACT, 1765

Source: Statutes at Large x. p. 18

Whereas, by an Act made in the last session of Parliament, several duties were granted, continued, and appropriated, towards defraying the expenses of defending, protecting, and securing, the British colonies and plantations in America: and whereas it is just and necessary, that provision be made for raising a further revenue within your Majesty's dominions in America, towards defraying the said expenses.... That from and after the first day of November, one thousand seven hundred and sixty-five, there shall be raised, levied, collected, and paid unto his Majesty, his heirs and successors, throughout the colonies and plantations in America which now are, or hereafter may be, under the dominion of his Majesty, his heirs and successors,

For every skin or piece of vellum or parchment, or sheet or

piece of paper, on which shall be ingrossed, written or printed, any declaration, pleas, replication, rejoinder, demurrer, or other pleading, or any copy thereof, in any court of law within the British colonies and plantations in America, a stamp duty of three pence. . . .

LVIII. And it is hereby further enacted . . . That all the forfeitures and penalties hereby inflicted, and which shall be incurred, in the said colonies and plantations, shall and may be prosecuted, sued for, and recovered in any court of record, or in any court of admiralty, in the respective colony or plantation where the offence shall be committed. . . .

4. THE DECLARATORY ACT, 1766

Although repealing the Stamp Act, the government passed the Declaratory Act to maintain its right to tax the colonies. In their rejoicing at the repeal of the hated Stamp Act the colonists largely failed to recognize the significance of this Act.

Source: Statutes at Large x. p. 152

Whereas several of the houses of representatives in his Majesty's colonies and plantations in America, have of late, and against law, claimed to themselves, or to the general assemblies of the same, the sole and exclusive right of imposing duties and taxes upon his Majesty's subjects in the said colonies and plantations; and have, in pursuance of such claim, passed certain votes, resolutions and orders, derogatory to the legislative authority of Parliament, and inconsistent with the dependency of the said colonies and plantations upon the Crown of Great Britain: may it therefore please your most excellent Majesty, that it may be declared, and be it declared by the King's most excellent Majesty, by and with the advice and consent of the Lords spiritual and temporal, and Commons, in this present Parliament assembled, and by the authority of the same, That the said colonies and plantations have been, are, and of right ought to be, subordinate unto, and dependent upon the imperial Crown and Parliament of Great Britain; and that the King's Majesty, by and with the advice and consent of the Lords spiritual and temporal, and Commons of Great Britain, in Parliament assembled, had, hath, and of right ought to have, full power and authority to make laws and statutes of sufficient force and validity to bind the colonies and people of America, subjects of the Crown of Great Britain, in all cases whatsoever.

II. And be it further declared and enacted by the authority aforesaid, That all resolutions, votes, orders, and proceedings, in any of the said colonies or plantations, whereby the power and authority of the Parliament of Great Britain, to make laws and statutes as aforesaid, is denied, or drawn into question, are, and are hereby declared to be, utterly null and void to all intents and purposes whatsoever.

5. THE AMERICAN TEA TRADE

Thomas Hutchinson, Governor of Massachusetts Bay, to Lord Hillsborough, the Secretary of State, 25 August, 1771.

Source: A. M. Schlesinger, *The Colonial Merchants and the American Revolution* (1918) p. 250.

The consumption of tea in America exceeds what anybody in England imagines. Some suppose five-sixths of the consumption in the last two years has been smuggled, and in Philadelphia and New York it is judged nine-tenths. The traders make such an extravagant profit that it will require more frequent seizures to discourage them than there is any reason to hope for. If the India Company had continued the sale of their teas at 2s 2d to 2s 4d, as they sold them two years ago, the Dutch trade would have been over by this time; but now that teas are 3s and upwards in England, the illicit trader can afford to lose one chest in three, whereas not one in a hundred has been seized. The Custom-house officers on shore have strong inducements to do their duty, being entitled to a proportion of one-third or more, but they are really afraid of the rage of the people. The sea officers have of late been more active, and Admiral Montague appears disposed to keep out his cruisers. Doubts, however, whether this trade will ever be discouraged in any other way than by reducing the price in England to the exporter very near the price it is at in Holland. For want of this, the revenue has lost, the last and present years, at least £60,000, sterling, from the 3d duty only. Believes the cruisers are capable of doing more. Suggests that a greater proportion is necessary for the particular officer who makes the seizure under a commission from the Customs than what he is now entitled to. Has discovered, when he has sworn some of the Navy officers to qualify them for their commissions from the Customs, a great indifference and disinclination to make themselves obnoxious to the people without any great advantage to themselves.

6. THE BOSTON TEA PARTY, 1773

Source: Calendar of Home Office Papers (1773–1775) p. 175

On the evening of 16th Dec., between 6 and 7 o'clock, a large mob assembled with axes, etc., encouraged by Mr John Hancock, Samuel Adams, and others, and marched in a body to where the ships lay, and there destroyed the whole by starting it into the sea. During the whole of this transaction neither the Governor, Magistrates, owners, nor Revenue officers ever called for the Admiral's assistance. If they had, he could easily have prevented the execution of the plan, but must have endangered the lives of many innocent people by firing on the town.

7. BURKE ON TAXATION OF THE AMERICAN COLONISTS, 1774

Source: Burke's Speech on American Taxation (ed. J. H. Moffatt, 1905) pp. 55–9

You understand, to be sure, that I speak of Charles Townshend, officially the reproducer of this fatal scheme. . . .

He had voted, and in the year 1765, had been an advocate for the Stamp Act. Things, and the disposition of men's minds, were changed. In short, the Stamp Act began to be no favourite in this House. He, therefore, attended at the private meeting, in which the resolutions moved by a right honourable gentleman were settled; resolutions leading to the repeal. The next day, he voted for that repeal; and he would have spoken for it, too, if an illness (not, as was then given out, a political), but, to my knowledge, a very real illness, had not prevented it. The very next session, as the fashion of this world passeth away, the repeal began to be in as bad an odour in this House as the Stamp Act had been in the session before. To conform to the temper which began to prevail, and to prevail mostly amongst those most in power, he declared, very early in the winter, that a revenue must be had out of America. Instantly he was tied down to his engagements by some who had no objection to such experiments at the cost of persons for whom they had no particular regard. The whole body of courtiers drove him onwards. They always talked as if the King stood in a sort of humiliated state, until something of the kind should be done. Here this extraordinary man, then Chancellor of the Exchequer, found himself in great straits. To please universally was the object of his life; but to tax and to please, no more than to love and to be wise, is not given to men. However, he attempted it. To render a tax palatable to the partisans of American revenue, he made a pre-amble, stating the necessity of such a revenue. To close with the American distinction, this revenue was external, or port duty; but again, to soften it to the other party, it was a duty of supply.

To gratify the colonists, it was laid on British manufactures, to satisfy the merchants of Britain, the duty was trivial, and (except that on tea, which touched only the devoted East India Company) on none of the grand objects of commerce. To counterwork the American contraband, the duty on tea was reduced from a shilling to threepence. But to secure the favour of those who would tax America, the scene of collection was changed, and, with the rest, it was levied in the colonies. What need I say more? This fine-spun scheme had the usual fate of all exquisite policy. But the original plan of the duties, and the mode of executing that plan, both arose singly and solely from a love of our applause. He was truly the child of the House. He never thought, did, or said anything, but with a view to you. He every day adapted himself to your disposition and adjusted himself before it as at a looking-glass. Hence arose this unfortunate Act.

Source: E. Burke, *Works* (1852) iii. pp. 289–91

I, for one, protest against compounding our demands: I declare against compounding for a poor limited sum, the immense, ever-growing, eternal debt, which is due to generous government from protected freedom. And so may I speed in the great object I propose to you, as I think it would not only be an act of injustice, but would be the worst economy in the world, to compel the colonies to a sum certain, either in the way of ransom, or in the way of compulsory compact.

But to clear up my ideas on this subject—a revenue from America transmitted hither—do not delude yourselves—you never can receive it—no, not a shilling. We have experience that from remote countries it is not to be expected. If, when you attempted to extract revenue from Bengal, you were obliged to return in loan what you had taken in imposition, what can you expect from North America? For certainly, if ever there was a country qualified to produce wealth, it is India; or an institution fitted for the transmission, it is the East India Company. America has none of these aptitudes. If America gives you taxable objects, on which you lay your duties here, and gives you, at the same time, a surplus by a foreign sale of her commodities to pay the duties on these objects, which you tax at home, she has performed her part to the British revenue. But with regard to her own internal establishments, she may, I doubt not she will, contribute in moderation. I say in moderation; for she ought not to be permitted to exhaust herself. She ought to be reserved to a war; the weight of which, with the enemies that we are most likely to have, must be considerable in her quarter of the globe. There she may serve you and serve you essentially.

For that service, for all service, whether of revenue, trade, or empire, my trust is in her interest in the British constitution. My hold of the colonies is in the close affection which grows from common names, from kindred blood, from similar privileges and equal protection. These are ties, which, though light as air, are as strong as links of iron. Let the colonies always keep the idea of their civil rights associated with your government; they will cling and grapple to you; and no force under heaven would be of power to tear them from their allegiance . . . As long as you have the wisdom to keep the sovereign authority of this country as the sanctuary of liberty, the sacred temple consecrated to our common faith, wherever the chosen race and sons of England worship freedom, they will turn their faces towards you . . . Deny them this participation of freedom, and you break that sole bond, which originally made, and must still preserve, the unity of the empire. Do not entertain so weak an imagination, as that your registers and your bonds, your affidavits and your sufferances, your cockets[1] and your clearances, are what form the great securities of your commerce. Do not dream that your letters of office, and your instructions, and your suspending clauses, are the things that hold together the great contexture of this mysterious whole. These things do not make your government. Dead instruments, passive tools as they are, it is the spirit of the English communion that gives all their life and efficacy to them. It is the spirit of the English constitution, which, infused through the mighty mass, pervades, feeds, unites, invigorates, vivifies every part of the empire, even down to the minutest member.

Is it not the same virtue which does everything for us here in England? Do you imagine then, that it is the land tax act, which raises your revenue? that it is the annual vote in the committee of supply, which gives you your army? or that it is the mutiny bill, which inspires it with bravery and discipline? No! surely no! It is the love of the people; it is their attachment to their government, from the sense of the deep stake they have in such a glorious institution, which gives you your army and your navy, and infuses into both that liberal obedience, without which your army would be a base rabble, and your navy nothing but rotten timber. . . .

We ought to elevate our minds to the greatness of that trust to which the order of Providence has called us. By adverting to the dignity of this high calling, our ancestors have turned a savage

[1]Certificates showing duty had been paid.

wilderness into a glorious empire; and have made the most extensive, and the only honourable conquests, not by destroying, but by promoting the wealth, the number, the happiness of the human race. Let us get an American revenue as we have got an American empire. English privileges have made it all that it is; English privileges alone will make it all it can be.

9. VIEWS OF THOMAS PAINE ON AMERICAN RELATIONS WITH BRITAIN

Source: 'Common Sense' in *The Political Works of Thomas Paine* (1842) p. 18

The sun never shone on a cause of greater worth. 'Tis not the affair of a city, a county, a province, or a kingdom, but of a continent—of at least one eighth part of the habitable globe. 'Tis not the concern of a day, a year, or an age; posterity are virtually involved in the contest, and will be more or less affected, even to the end of time, by the proceedings now. Now is the seed-time of continental union, faith and honour. The least fracture now will be like a name engraved with the point of a pin on the tender rind of a young oak; the wound will enlarge with the tree, and posterity read it in full grown characters. . . . I have heard it asserted by some, that as America hath flourished under her former connection with Great Britain, that the same connection is necessary towards her future happiness, and will always have the same effect. Nothing can be more fallacious than this kind of argument. We may as well assert that because a child has thriven upon milk, that it is never to have meat, or that the first twenty years of our lives is to become a precedent for the next twenty. But even this is admitting more than is true, for I answer roundly, that America would have flourished as much, and probably much more, had no European power had anything to do with her. The commerce by which she hath enriched herself, are the necessaries of life, and will always have a market while eating is the custom of Europe.

But she has protected us, say some. That she has engrossed us is true, and defended the continent at our expense as well as her own, is admitted and she would have defended Turkey from the same motive, viz. the sake of trade and dominion.

Alas, we have been long led away by ancient prejudices; and made large sacrifices to superstition. We have boasted the protection of Great Britain, without considering that her motive was interest not attachment; that she did not protect us from our enemies on our account, but from her enemies on her own account, from those who had no quarrel with us on any other account, and who will always be our enemies on the same account. Let Britain waive her pretensions to the continent, or the continent throw off the dependence, and we should be at peace with France and Spain were they at war with Britain. The miseries of Hanover last war ought to warn us against connections . . . But Britain is the parent country, say some. Then the more shame upon her conduct. Even brutes do not devour their young, nor savages make war upon their families; wherefore the assertion, if true, turns to her reproach; but it happens not to be true, or only partly so, and the phrase parent or mother country hath been jesuitically adopted by the King and his parasites with a low papistical design of gaining an unfair bias on the credulous weakness of our minds. Europe, and not England, is the parent country of America. This new world hath been the asylum for the persecuted lovers of civil and religious liberty from every part of Europe . . . Not one-third of the inhabitants, even of this province, are of English descent. Wherefore I reprobate the phrase of parent or mother country applied to England only as being false, selfish, narrow, and ungenerous. . . .

I challenge the warmest advocate for reconciliation, to show a single advantage that this continent can reap, by being connected with Great Britain. I repeat the challenge, not a single advantage is derived. Our corn will fetch its price in any market in Europe, and our imported goods must be paid for, buy them where we will.

But the injuries and disadvantages we sustain by that connection, are without number; and our duty to mankind at large, as well as to ourselves, instruct us to renounce the alliance: because, any submission to, or dependence on Great Britain, tends directly to involve this continent in European wars and quarrels; and set us at variance with nations, who would otherwise seek our friendship, and against whom we have neither anger nor complaint. As Europe is our market for trade, we ought to form no partial connection with any part of it. It is the true interest of America to steer clear of European contentions, which she never can do, while by her dependence on Britain, she is made the make-weight in the scale of British politics. . . .

. . . As to government matters, it is not in the power of Britain to do this continent justice: the business of it will soon be too weighty, and intricate, to be managed with any tolerable degree of convenience, by a power so distant from us, and so very ignorant of us; for if they cannot conquer us, they cannot govern us. To be always running three or four thousand miles with a tale or a petition, waiting four or five months for an answer, which when obtained required five or six more to explain it in, will in a few years be looked upon as folly and childishness. There was a time when it was proper, and there is a proper time for it to cease. . . .

. . . I am not induced by motives of pride, party, or resentment to espouse the doctrine of separation and independence; I am clearly, positively, and conscientiously persuaded, that it is the true interest of this continent to be so; that everything short of that is mere patchwork, that it can afford no lasting felicity, that it is leaving the sword to our children, and shrinking back at a time, when, a little more, a little farther, would have rendered this continent the glory of the earth.

10. THE BATTLE OF LEXINGTON, 1775

i. *The American official account*

> Source: H. Niles, *Principles and Acts of the Revolution* (1822) p. 434

Watertown, April 26, 1775

In provincial congress of Massachusetts, to the inhabitants of Great Britain.

Friends and fellow subjects—Hostilities are at length commenced in this colony by the troops under the command of General Gage, and it being of the greatest importance, that an early, true, and authentic account of this inhuman proceeding should be known to you, the congress of this colony have transmitted the same, and from want of a session of the hon. continental congress, think it proper to address you on the alarming occasion.

By the clearest depositions relative to this transaction, it will appear that on the night preceding the nineteenth of April instant, a body of the King's troops, under the command of Colonel Smith, were secretly landed at Cambridge, with an apparent design to take or destroy the military and other stores, provided for the defence of this colony, and deposited at Concord—that some inhabitants of the colony, on the night aforesaid, whilst travelling peaceably on the road, between Boston and Concord, were seized and greatly abused by armed men, who appeared to be officers of General Gage's army; that the town of Lexington, by these means, was alarmed, and a company of the inhabitants mustered on the occasion —that the regular troops on their way to Concord, marched into the said town of Lexington, and the said company, on their approach, began to disperse—that, notwithstanding this, the regulars rushed on with great violence, and first began hostilities, by firing on said Lexington company, whereby they killed eight, and wounded several others—that the regulars continued their fire, until those of said company, who were neither killed nor wounded, had made their escape—that Colonel Smith, with the detachment then marched to Concord, where a number of provincials were again fired on by the troops, two of them killed and several wounded, before the provincials fired on them, and provincials were again fired on by the troops, produced an engagement that lasted through the day, in which many of the provincials and more of the regular troops were killed and wounded.

To give a particular account of the ravages of the troops, as they retreated from Concord to Charlestown, would be very difficult if not impracticable; let it suffice to say, that a great number of the houses on the road were plundered and rendered unfit for use, several were burnt, women in child-bed were driven by the soldiery naked into the streets, old men peaceably in their houses were shot dead, and such scenes exhibited as would disgrace the annals of the most uncivilized nation. . . .

By order,
Joseph Warren, President

ii. *The English version—Lt. Col. Smith's report to General Gage*

Source: Massachusetts Historical Society, *Proceedings* (1876) p. 350

Sir,—In obedience to your Excellency's commands, I marched on the evening of the 18th inst. with the corps of grenadiers and light infantry for Concord, to execute your Excellency's orders with respect to destroying all ammunition, artillery, tents, etc., collected there, which was effected. . . . Notwithstanding we marched with utmost expedition and secrecy, we found the country had intelligence or strong suspicion of our coming, and fired many signal guns, and rung the alarm bells repeatedly; and were informed, when at Concord, that some cannon had been taken out of the town that day, that others, with some stores, had been carried three days before, which prevented our having an opportunity of destroying so much as might have been expected at our first setting off.

I think it proper to observe, that when I had got some miles on the march from Boston, I detached six light infantry companies to march with all expedition to seize the two bridges on different roads beyond Concord. On these companies' arrival at Lexington, I understand from the report of Major Pitcairn, who was with them, and from many officers, that they found on a green close to the road a body of the country people drawn up in military order, with arms and accoutrements, and, as appeared after, loaded; and that they had posted some men in a dwelling and Meeting-house. Our troops advanced towards them, without any intention of injuring them, further than to inquire the reason of their being thus assembled, and, if not satisfactory, to have secured their arms; but they in confusion went off, principally to the left, only one of them fired before he went off, and three or four more jumped over a wall and fired from behind it among the soldiers; on which the troops returned it, and killed several of them. They likewise fired on the soldiers from the Meeting and dwelling-houses. . . . Rather earlier than this, on the road, a countryman from behind a wall had snapped his piece at Lieutenants Adair and Sutherland, but it flashed and did not go off. After this we saw some in the woods, but marched on to Concord without anything further happening. While at Concord we saw vast numbers assembling in many parts; at one of the bridges they marched down, with a very considerable body, on the light infantry posted there. On their coming pretty near, one of our men fired on them, which they returned; on which an action ensued, and some few were killed and wounded. In this affair, it appears that, after the bridge was quitted, they scalped and otherwise ill-treated one or two of the men who were either killed or severely wounded . . . On our leaving Concord to return to Boston, they began to fire on us from behind the walls, ditches, trees, etc., which, as we marched, increased to a very great degree, and continued without intermission of five minutes altogether, for, I believe, upwards of eighteen miles; so that I can't think but it must have been a preconcerted scheme in them, to attack the King's troops the first favourable opportunity that offered, other-wise, I think they could not, in so short a time from our marching out, have raised such a numerous body, and for so great a space of ground. Notwithstanding the enemy's numbers, they did not make one gallant attempt during so long an action, though our men were so very much fatigued, but kept under cover.

I have the honour etc.

F. Smith, Lieutenant-Colonel 10th Foot

iii. *Source:* R. W. Emerson, *Hymn Sung at the Completion of the Concord Monument*

> By the rude bridge that arched the flood,
> Their flag to April's breeze unfurled
> Here once the embattled farmers stood,
> And fired the shot heard round the world.

11. THE DECLARATION OF INDEPENDENCE, 1776

Source: F. N. Thorpe, *Federal & State Constitutions* i. p. 3

In Congress, July 4, 1776

THE UNANIMOUS DECLARATION OF THE THIRTEEN UNITED STATES OF AMERICA

When in the course of human events, it becomes necessary for one people to dissolve the political bands which have connected them with another, and to assume among the Powers of the earth, the separate and equal station to which the Laws of Nature and of Nature's God entitle them, a decent respect to the opinions of mankind requires that they should declare the causes which impel them to the separation.

We hold these truths to be self-evident, that all men are created equal, that they are endowed by their Creator with certain un-alienable rights, that among these are Life, Liberty and the pursuit of Happiness. That to secure these rights, governments are insti-tuted among men, deriving their just powers from the consent of the governed. That whenever any form of government becomes destructive of these ends, it is the Right of the People to alter or to abolish it, and to institute new government, laying its foundation on such principles and organizing its powers in such form, as to them shall seem most likely to effect their safety and happiness. Prudence, indeed, will dictate that governments long established should not be changed for light and transient causes; and accordingly all experience hath shown, that mankind are more disposed to suffer, while evils are sufferable, than to right themselves by abolishing the forms to which they are accustomed. But when a long train of abuses and usurpations, pursuing invariably the same object evinces a design to reduce them under absolute despotism, it is their right, it is their duty, to throw off such government, and to provide new guards for their future security. Such has been the patient sufferance of these Colonies; and such is now the necessity which constrains them to alter their former systems of government. The history of the present King of Great Britain is a history of repeated injuries and usurpations, all having in direct object the establishment of an absolute tyranny over these States. To prove this, let facts be submitted to a candid world. . . .

[Here follows a list of the grievances of the colonies]

. . . We, therefore, the Representatives of the united States of America, in General Congress, assembled, appealing to the Supreme Judge of the world for the rectitude of our intentions, do, in the Name, and by Authority of the good People of these Colonies, solemnly publish and declare, That these United Colonies are, and of right ought to be free and independent States; that they are absolved from all allegiance to the British Crown, and that all political connection between them and the State of Great Britain, is and ought to be totally dissolved; and that as free and independent States, they have full power to levy war, conclude peace, contract alliances, establish commerce, and to do all other acts and things which independent States may of right do. And for the support of this Declaration, with a firm reliance on the Protection of Divine Providence, we mutually pledge to each other our lives, our fortunes and our sacred honour.

12. WASHINGTON EXHORTS HIS ARMY, 1776

Source: J. Sparks, *Life of George Washington* (1837) ii. p. 347

August 23rd, 1776

The enemy have now landed on Long Island, and the hour is fast approaching on which the honour and success of this army and the safety of our bleeding country will depend. Remember, officers and soldiers, that you are freemen, fighting for the blessings of liberty; that slavery will be your portion, and that of your posterity if you do not acquit yourselves like men. Remember how your courage and spirit have been traduced by your cruel invaders; though they have found by dear experience at Boston, Charlestown, and other places, what a few brave men contending in their land and in the best of causes, can do against hirelings and mercenaries. Be cool but determined; do not fire at a distance, but wait for orders from your officers. It is the General's express orders that if any man attempt to skulk, lie down or retreat without orders, he be instantly shot down as an example. He hopes no such will be found in this army; but on the contrary, that every one for himself resolving to conquer or die, and trusting in the smiles of heaven upon so good a cause, will behave with bravery and resolution. Those who are distinguished for their gallantry and good conduct may depend on being honourably noticed and suitably rewarded; and if this army will but emulate and imitate their brave country-men in other parts of America, he has no doubt they will by a glorious victory save their country, and acquire to themselves immortal honour.

Source: Report of the Earl of Chatham's last speech, from the *London Magazine* (1778) xlvii. pp. 213–14

He [Chatham] appeared to be extremely feeble, and spoke with that difficulty of utterance which is the characteristic of severe indisposition. His Lordship began with declaring that his ill health had for some time obliged him to absent himself from the performance of his parliamentary duty; he rejoiced, however, that he was yet alive to give his vote against so impolitic, so inglorious a measure as the acknowledgment of the independency of America; and declared he would much rather be in his grave than see the lustre of the British throne tarnished, the dignity of the empire disgraced, the glory of the nation sunk to such a degree as it must be, when the dependency of America on the sovereignty of Great Britain was given up. The Earl next adverted to the conduct of the Court of France, and observed, that at a crisis like the present, he would openly speak his sentiments, although they might turn out to be dangerous. As a reason for throwing off reserve, he said he did not approve of halting between two opinions, when there was no middle path; that it was necessary absolutely to declare either for peace or war, and when the former could not be preserved with honour, the latter ought to be declared without hesitation. Having made this remark, he asked, where was the ancient spirit of the nation, that a foreign power was suffered to bargain for that commerce which was her natural right, and enter into a treaty with her own subjects, without instantly resenting it? Could it be possible that we were the same people who but fifteen years ago were the envy and admiration of all the world? How were we altered! and what had made the alteration? He feared there was something in the dark, something lurking near the throne, which gave motion to administration—something unseen, which caused such pusillanimous, such timid, such dastardly councils. What! were we to sit down in an ignominious tameness? to say, 'Take from us what you will, but in God's name let us be at peace?' Were we blinded by despair? Could we forget that we were Englishmen? Could we forget that the nation had stood the Danish irruptions? had stood the irruptions of other nations! had stood the inroads of the Scotch! had stood the Norman conquests! had stood the threatened invasion by the famous Spanish armada, and the various efforts of the Bourbon compacts! Why, then, should we now give up all, without endeavouring to prevent our losses, without a blow, without an attempt to resent the insults offered us? If France and Spain were for war, why not try an issue with them? If we fell afterwards, we should fall decently, and like men.

RELIGIOUS, ECONOMIC
and
SOCIAL

Religion

i. *The Relief of the Dissenters*

The government found a solution to the dilemma related below by passing an Indemnity Act annually after 1727.

Source: Lord Hervey, *Memoirs of the Reign of George II* (1848) i. pp. 144–6

The Dissenters' plea for asking this favour of the Parliament [the repeal of the Test and Corporation Acts] seemed very natural and reasonable; they said they had for above forty years shown themselves steady friends to the constitution of England in the State, and constant supporters of the established government on Revolution principles; they had served hitherto without any reward, and now desired no other gratuity than the bare removal of that unjust distinction made between them and the rest of their fellow-subjects under which they had so long laboured and by which they were excluded from all employments of trust or profit. They said what made this request more reasonable was, that the hardship they now complained of had never been laid upon them all, had they not originally consented to it themselves, and that the reason of their consenting to it had been merely for the public good and the common Protestant cause; circumstances at that time requiring their voluntary submission to this self-denial act in order to facilitate the exclusion of Papists from all places of power when this kingdom was on the brink of being subjected to their sway under the authority of a Popish successor. They further added that they had not only always shown themselves unwavering and indefatigable champions for the Protestant succession, but that they had equally proved themselves firm and constant friends to what was called the Whig party, and the set of men now in power; consequently, if they could not get rid of this stigmatizing brand of reproach that declared them unfit to be trusted with any employment in the executive part of the civil government under a Whig Parliament, they could never hope for relief at all, since the other set of men, who called themselves the Church party, and whom they had always opposed, should they come into power, would not only from principle forbear to show the Dissenters any favour, but would certainly from resentment go still further, and probably load them with some new oppression. . . .

. . . This design of the Presbyterians put the Administration under great difficulties and into great apprehensions; they saw the injustice of opposing their petition if it came into Parliament, and the danger there was, on the other hand, of showing it any countenance; they knew it would seem the last ingratitude in any who called themselves Whigs to reject it, and the highest imprudence to receive it; for though the clergy had hitherto been kept pretty quiet by nothing being attempted either to restrain their power or to favour their adversaries, yet the ministers were sure that if any step was taken that looked like encouragement to the Dissenters, it would inevitably turn all the parsons, to a man, in the approaching elections, against every one that should appear to forward it, and as to those who did not forward it, the [Dissenting] ministers would never give them a vote again. . . .

ii. *The Growth of Methodism*

1. These are but two of the many occasions when John Wesley travelled and preached in danger of his life.

Source: *The Journals of John Wesley* (1827) i. pp. 418, 483–5

(*a*) Thursday, October 20, 1743 . . . we had not gone a hundred yards when the mob of Walsall came pouring in, like a flood, and bore down all before them. The Darlaston mob made what defence they could; but they were weary as well as out-numbered; so that, in a short time, many being knocked down, the rest ran away, and left me in their hands.

To attempt speaking was vain; for the noise on every side was like the roaring of the sea; so they dragged me along till we came to the town, where seeing the door of a large house open, I attempted to go in; but a man, catching me by the hair, pulled me back into the middle of the mob. They made no more stop till they had carried me through the main street, from one end of the town to the other. I continued speaking all the time to those within hearing, feeling no pain or weariness. At the west end of the town, seeing a door half open, I made toward it, and would have gone in; but a gentleman in the shop would not suffer me, saying, 'They would pull the house down to the ground.' However, I stood at the door, and asked, 'Are you willing to hear me speak?' Many cried out, 'No, no! knock his brains out; down with him; kill him at once.' Others said, 'Nay, but we will hear him first.' I began asking, 'What evil have I done? Which of you all have I wronged in word or deed?' and continued speaking for above a quarter of an hour, till my voice suddenly failed; then the floods began to lift up their voice again; many crying out, 'Bring him away; bring him away.'

In the meantime my strength and my voice returned, and I broke out aloud into prayer. And now the man who just before headed the mob, turned and said, 'Sir, I will spend my life for you; follow me, and not one soul here shall touch a hair of your head.' Two or three of his fellows confirmed his words, and got close to me immediately; at the same time the gentleman in the shop cried out, 'For shame, for shame; let him go.' An honest butcher, who was a little farther off, said, 'It was a shame they should do thus'; and pulled back four or five, one after another, who were running on the most fiercely. The people then, as if it had been by common consent, fell back to the right and left; while those three or four men took me between them, and carried me through them all. But on the bridge the mob rallied again; we, therefore, went on one side, over the Mill-dam, and thence through the meadows, till a little before ten God brought me safe to Wednesbury; having lost only one flap of my waistcoat, and a little skin from one of my hands.

(*b*) Thursday, July 4, 1745—I rode to Falmouth. About three in the afternoon I went to see a gentlewoman who had long been indisposed. Almost as soon as I was set down, the house was beset on all sides by an innumerable multitude of people. A louder or more confused noise could hardly be at the taking of a city by storm. At first, Mrs B. and her daughter tried to quiet them. But it was labour lost. They might as well have attempted to still the raging of the sea. They were soon glad to shift for themselves, and leave K.E. and me to do as well as we could. The rabble roared with all their throats, 'Bring out the Canorum! Where is the Canorum?' an unmeaning word which the Cornish generally used instead of Methodist. No answer being given, they quickly forced open the outer door, and filled the passage. Only a wainscot partition was between us which was not likely to stand long. I immediately took down a large looking-glass which hung against it, supposing the whole side would fall in at once.

When they began their work with abundance of bitter imprecations, poor Kitty was utterly astonished, and cried out, 'O Sir, what must we do?' I said, 'We must pray.' Indeed at that time, to all appearance, our lives were not worth an hour's purchase. She asked, 'But, Sir, is it not better for you to hide yourself? To get into the cupboard?' I answered, 'No. It is better for me to stand just where I am.' Among those without, were the crews of some privateers, which were lately come into the harbour. Some of these, being angry at the slowness of the rest, thrust them away, and coming up altogether, set their shoulders to the inner door, and cried out, 'Avast, lads, avast!' Away went all the hinges at once, and the door fell back into the room.

I stepped forward at once into the midst of them and said, 'Here I am. Which of you has anything to say to me? To which of you have I done wrong? To you? Or you? Or you?' I continued speaking, till I came, bare-headed as I was (for I purposely left my hat, that they might all see my face) into the middle of the street, and then raising my voice, said, 'Neighbours, countrymen! Do you desire to hear me speak?' They cried vehemently, 'Yes, yes, he shall speak, he shall, nobody shall hinder him.' But having nothing to stand on, and no advantage of the ground, I could be heard by few only. However, I spoke without intermission, and as far as the sound reached, the people were still; till one or two of their captains turned about and swore, 'Not a man should touch him'. . . .

. . . I never saw before, no, not at Walsall itself, the hand of God so plainly shown as here. There I had many companions, who were willing to die with me; here not a friend, but one simple girl;

who likewise was hurried away from me in an instant, as soon as ever she came out of Mrs B's door. There I received some blows, lost part of my clothes, and was covered over with dirt. Here, although the hands of perhaps some hundreds of people were lifted up to strike or throw, yet they were one and all stopped in the mid-way, so that not a man touched me with one of his fingers. Neither was anything thrown from first to last; so that I had not even a speck of dirt on my clothes. Who can deny, that God heareth the prayer? Or that He hath all power in heaven and earth?

I took boat at about half an hour past five. Many of the mob waited at the end of the town, who seeing me escaped out of their hands, could only revenge themselves with their tongues. But a few of the fiercest ran along the shore, to receive me at my landing. I walked up the steep, narrow passage from the sea, at the top of which the foremost man stood. I looked him in the face and said, 'I wish you a good night.' He spake not, nor moved hand or foot till I was on horseback. Then he said, 'I wish you was in hell'; and turned back to his companions.

2.   The preaching of George Whitefield.

Source: Hist. MSS. Comm: Diary of the 1st Earl of Egmont iii. pp. 67–9

Friday, 8 June, 1739

The Reverend Mr Whitefield who has for some days been preaching in this neighbourhood, sent my wife word that he would preach [as requested] . . . About six, a stage being erected for him, he came to our house to return our civility to him, and soon after mounted the stage, which was placed so conveniently that we heard him with great ease out of our summer house window, where we invited our neighbours to partake of the curiosity.

The multitude, about 200, being assembled, he began with the hundredth psalm, which numbers joined in. Then he made a long pathetic prayer, and lastly, began his sermon with a clear and audible voice. The subject of it was the necessity of the being born again, or the new birth. . . . He preached by heart with much earnestness, and spreading his arms wide, and was at no loss for matter or words, and the people were very attentive. . . .

I took notice to him of his preaching in the fields, and not only in churches; he answered, he should choose to preach in churches, but that he was excluded, but was not sorry because it gave an opportunity to many to hear him who never came to church, and these are the more reprobate sort, who, though they came out of curiosity, may possibly be touched by his discourses and converted. Besides, Dissenters, who of course will not enter our churches, do willingly hear him in the field. That some clergymen call him a dissenter and schismatic, but what would they have him do? They shut him out of their churches, and constrain him to take this method, for he is bound to preach the Gospel, being ordained to that purpose.

❖

Agriculture

I. ENCLOSURE

i. *Enclosure by Private Act of Parliament, 1766*
    Source: Commons' Journals (1765–6) xxx. pp. 459 ff

A Petition of Stephen Croft, the Younger, Esquire, Lord of the manor of Stillington, in the county of York, and owner of several estates, within the said manor and parish of Stillington, and also Impropriator of the Great Tithes there; of the Reverend James Worsley, Clerk, Prebendary of the Prebend of Stillington aforesaid, patron of the Vicarage of Stillington aforesaid, of the Reverend Lawrence Sterne, Clerk, Vicar of the said parish, and of William Stainforth, Esquire, and of several other persons, whose names are thereunto subscribed, being also owners of copyhold messuages, cottages, estates, and other properties, within the said parish; was presented to the House and read; setting forth, that, within the said manor and parish, is a common, or waste, called Stillington

Common, and also open fields and ings,[1] which, in their present situation, are incapable of improvement; and that it would be of great advantage to the several persons interested in the said common, fields and ings, if they were enclosed and divided into specific allotments, and all rights of common and average thereon, or upon any other commonable lands in the said parish, were extinguished, or if the said common was so enclosed, and a power given to the several proprietors and owners of estates in the said fields and ings, to flat and enclose the same, first making satisfaction to the impropriator upon the tithes thereof; and after the flatting and enclosing the same, all right of common, or average, was to cease; and therefore praying, that leave may be given to bring in a Bill for the purposes aforesaid, or any of them, in such manner, and under such regulations, as the House shall deem meet.

Ordered, That leave be given to bring in a Bill pursuant to the prayer of the said petition; and that Mr Cholmley, Sir George Savile, and Sir Joseph Mawbey, do prepare and bring in the same.

[February 3. Bill presented to the House and read a first time]

February 10, 1766. A Bill for enclosing and dividing the common waste grounds, open fields, open meadows, grounds, and ings, within the parish of Stillington, in the county of York, was read a second time.

Resolved. That the Bill be committed to Mr Cholmley, Mr Fonerau, Sir John Taines [and others]; and all the members who serve for the counties of York, Nottingham, Northumberland, and Durham: and they are to meet this afternoon, at five of the clock, in the Speaker's Chamber.

February 27. Mr Cholmley reported from the Committee, to whom the Bill for enclosing and dividing the common waste grounds [etc.] within the parish of Stillington, in the county of York, was committed. That the Committee had examined the allegations of the Bill; and found the same to be true; and that the parties concerned had given their consent to the Bill, to the satisfaction of the Committee, except the proprietors of sixty acres of land in the said fields and ings, who refused their consent to the enclosure, and the proprietors of twenty seven acres of land, who were not at home when application was made for their consents;

[1] Meadows.

and that the whole of the said fields and ings contain six hundred acres or thereabouts; and also, except the proprietors of eight common rights, who refused to consent, and the proprietors of seven common rights, who were from home when application was made for their consents; and that the whole number of common rights are eighty-nine; and that no person appeared before the Committee to oppose the Bill; and that the Committee had gone through the Bill, and made several amendments thereunto; which they had directed him to report to the House; and he read the report in his place; and afterwards delivered the Bill with the amendments, in at the Clerk's Table; where the amendments were once read throughout; and then a second time, one by one; and upon the Question severally put thereon, were agreed to by the House; and several amendments were made, by the House, to the Bill. Ordered, that the Bill, with the amendments be ingrossed.

ii. *A Petition against Enclosure*

Source: Commons' Journals (1792) lii. p. 661

A Petition of the hereunder-signed small Proprietors of Land and Persons entitled to Rights of Common [at Raunds, Northamptonshire].

That the petitioners beg leave to represent to the House that, under the pretence of improving lands in the same parish, the cottagers and other persons entitled to right of common on the lands intended to be enclosed, will be deprived of an inestimable privilege, which they now enjoy, of turning a certain number of their cows, calves and sheep, on and over the said lands; a privilege that enables them not only to maintain themselves and their families in the depth of winter, when they cannot, even for their money, obtain from the occupiers of other lands the smallest portion of milk or whey for such necessary purpose, but in addition to this, they can now supply the grazier with young or lean stock at a reasonable price to fatten and bring to market at a more moderate rate for general consumption, which they conceive to be the most rational and effectual way of establishing public plenty and cheapness of provision; and they further conceive, that a more ruinous effect of this enclosure will be the almost total depopulation of their town, now filled with bold and hardy husbandmen, from among whom, and the inhabitants of other open parishes, the nation has hitherto derived its greatest strength and glory, in the supply of its fleets and armies, and driving them, from necessity and want of employ, in vast crowds, into manufacturing towns, where the very nature of their employment, over the loom or the forge, soon may waste their strength, and consequently debilitate their posterity, and by imperceptible degrees obliterate that great principle of obedience to the Laws of God and their country, which forms the character of the simple and artless villagers, more equally distributed through the open counties, and on which so much depends the good order and government of the state. These are some of the injuries to themselves as individuals, and of the ill consequences to the public, which the petitioners conceive will follow from this, as they have already done from many enclosures, but which they did not think they were entitled to lay before the House (the constitutional patron and protector of the poor) until it unhappily came to their own lot to be exposed to them through the Bill now pending.

iii. *An Official Justification of Enclosure*

   Source: Survey of the Board of Agriculture for Somersetshire (1798) pp. 48–50, 52

Let us begin with taking a view of the objections which have been stated to this species of improvement, and see if we cannot prove them to be for the most part either false or frivolous.

   1st. Invasion of the rights and interest of the cottagers.

The foremost of these objections carries with it the appearance of a humane attention to the comfort of the poor; but a brief investigation will lessen its influence, if not totally refute it.

There are but two modes of enclosing commons. First by unanimous consent of the parties claiming rights, who delegate power to commissioners, chosen by themselves, to ascertain their validity, and divide them accordingly, under covenants and agreements properly drawn and executed for the purpose. Or secondly, by Act of Parliament obtained by the petition of a certain proportion of the commoners, both in number and value, whereby a minority, sanctioned only by ignorance, prejudice, or selfishness, is precluded from defeating the ends of private advantage and public utility.

In point of economy, the first of these methods is most eligible, as it saves the expense of an Act of Parliament, with an equal security to the proprietors. But it is seldom practised unless in commons on a small scale, from the difficulty of procuring the consent of every individual claimant, without which it cannot be accomplished.

In either of these methods, it is manifest that the right of the cottager cannot be invaded; since with respect to legal or equitable construction, he stands precisely on the same ground with his more opulent neighbours; and as to his interest, I can truly declare that, in all cases which have fallen within my observation, enclosures have meliorated his condition, by exciting a spirit of activity and industry, whereby habits of sloth have been by degrees overcome, and supineness and inactivity have been exchanged for vigour and exertion.

Besides, moral effects of an injurious tendency accrue to the cottager from a reliance on the imaginary benefits of stocking a common. The possession of a cow or two, with a hog, and a few geese, naturally exalts the peasant, in his own conception, above his brothers in the same rank of society. It inspires some degree of confidence in a property, inadequate to his support. In sauntering after his cattle, he acquires a habit of indolence. Quarter, half, and occasionally whole days are imperceptibly lost. Day labour becomes disgusting; the aversion increases by indulgence; and at length the sale of a half-fed calf, or hog, furnishes the means of adding intemperance to idleness. The sale of a cow frequently succeeds, and its wretched and disappointed possessor, unwilling to resume the daily and regular course of labour, from whence he drew his former subsistence, by various modes of artifice and imposition, exacts from the poor's rate the relief to which he is in no degree entitled.

iv. *Arthur Young's Attack upon Enclosure*

Source: A. Young, *An Inquiry into the Propriety of Applying Wastes etc.* (1801) pp. 42, 13

(*a*) I will not dispute their meaning [the purpose of enclosers]; but the poor look to facts, not meanings; and the fact is, that by nineteen enclosure bills in twenty they are injured, in some grossly injured. It may be said that commissioners are sworn to do justice. What is that to the people who suffer? It must be generally known that they suffer in their own opinions, and yet enclosures go on by commissioners, who dissipate the poor people's cows wherever they come, as well those kept legally as those which are not. What is it to the poor man to be told that the Houses of Parliament are extremely tender of property, while the father of the family is forced to sell his cow and his land because the one is not competent to the other; and being deprived of the only motive to industry, squanders the money, contracts bad habits, enlists for a soldier, and leaves the wife and children to the parish? If enclosures were beneficial to the poor, rates would not rise as in other parishes after an act to enclose. The poor in these parishes may say, and with truth, Parliament may be tender of property; all I know is, I had a cow, and Act of Parliament has taken it from me. And thousands may make this speech with truth.

(*b*) Go to an alehouse kitchen of an old enclosed country, and there you will see the origin of poverty and poor rates. For whom are they to be sober? For whom are they to save? (Such are their questions) For the parish? If I am diligent, shall I have leave to build a cottage? If I am sober, shall I have land for a cow? If I am frugal, shall I have half an acre of potatoes? You offer no motives; you have nothing but a parish officer and a workhouse! Bring me another pot.

2. IMPROVEMENT AND EXPERIMENT

Plates 30 and 31

i. Source: A. Young, *The Farmer's Tour* (1771) ii. p. 150

As I shall presently leave Norfolk it will not be improper to give a slight review of the husbandry which has rendered the name of this county so famous in the farming world. Pointing out the practices which have succeeded so nobly here, may perhaps be of some use to other countries possessed of the same advantages, but unknowing in the art to use them.

From forty to fifty years ago, all the northern and western, and a part of the eastern tracts of the county, were sheep walks, let so low as from 6d to 1s 6d and 2s an acre. Much of it was in this condition only thirty years ago. The great improvements have been made by means of the following circumstances.

First. By enclosing without the assistance of Parliament
Second. By a spirited use of marl and clay
Third. By the introduction of an excellent course of crops
Fourth. By the culture of turnips well hand-hoed
Fifth. By the culture of clover and ray-grass
Sixth. By landlords granting long leases
Seventh. By the country being divided chiefly into large farms.

ii. *Marling*

Source: A. Young, *A Six Weeks' Tour* (1768) pp. 23–4

. . . The principal farms (at least those that are most commonly mentioned) [in this part of Norfolk] are Mr Curtis's of Sommerfield, 2,500 acres. Mr Mallet's of Dunton, as much. Mr Barton's of Rougham, 3,000. Messrs. Glover's of Creek and Barwic. Messrs. Savary's of Sydderstone, and Mr Rogerson's of Narford, each 1100 acres. Cultivation in all its branches is carried on by these men, and many others, in a very complete manner. But marling is the great foundation of their wealth.

They lay about 100 loads on an acre, which cost them for digging from £1 5s to £1 10s and they reckon the expenses of the team, and other labour, to be as much more. The improvement lasts in great vigour above twenty years; and the land is always the better for it. Their course of crops is—Marl, and break up for wheat. 2. Turnips. 3. Barley. 4. Laid down with clover and ryegrass for three years, or sometimes only two. They dung or fold for all their winter-corn, and reckon two nights fold equal to a

dunging; the quantity of the latter they lay upon an acre is 12 loads.
For some years after the marling, they reap, on a medium, four
quarters of wheat per acre, and five of barley; and 15 or 18 years
after marling, three quarters of wheat, and four and a half of soft
corn. . . .

iii. *Moorland*

Source: A. Young, *A Six Months' Tour through the North of England*
(1770) ii. pp. 212–14

. . . Mr Thomas Elliot of Fremington is one of the greatest
improvers of moors in Yorkshire. . . .

His design was to enclose and improve a field every year; and
this he accordingly has executed annually for several years. The
method he takes to improve the black moory land is this.

He first pares and burns and limes it; and sows it with turnips;
of which he gets a pretty good crop, worth on an average, about
40s an acre. The next year he sows turnips again, and gets a second
crop equally valuable with the first. After this, he lays down to
grass with ray grass, clover, hay-feeds, etc. etc. He has tried some
alone, and some with oats, both do equally well, but the clover
much the worst; the climate he apprehends too cold for it. He often
limes for every crop. The oats are frequently five quarters per acre.

Potatoes he also cultivates in this black soil, in rows two feet
asunder, and the sets one foot, and of these he gets often 100
bushels per acre.

The grass turns out very good profitable pasture, keeps milch
cows, horses, small fatting beasts, sheep etc., very well. Two
acres of it will carry a cow through the summer well. Some of these
grass enclosures are five years old, and rather improve than decay;
being better now than at first after laying.

Some pieces of this black land which he has enclosed wanted
draining; and he has drained such effectually, by drains two feet
and an half wide at top; two feet and an half deep, and one foot
wide at bottom: the black earth thrown out he mixes with lime,
and finds it an excellent compost, which answers greatly.

This black land in its unimproved state, is worth to no tenant

above 1s 6d an acre, but improved as above, would let very easily
for 3s....

iv. *Grasses*

Young speaks of this improving landlord as being 'known all over
Europe as one of the most accurate of cultivators'.

Source: ibid. pp. 28–9

... I [Sir Digby Legard of Ganton, Yorks] have enclosed 300
acres on the top of the wolds, and have laid down the greatest part
with various kinds of grasses. Sainfoine makes the most general
improvement, but it does not succeed in all parts alike, and indeed
in some will not do at all; where the soil is shallowest and most
stony or gravelly, it prospers best. The greatest part of my sainfoine
is drilled in rows a foot asunder, this takes but half the feed, and
brings as good a crop as that which is sowed broad-cast. White
clover, rye-grass, rib-grass, and burnet, succeed pretty well with
me, these grasses taken at an average, a good year with a bad one,
and 30 or 40 acres together, yield near a ton of hay per acre, on
land which never bore any hay before it was enclosed: I esteem
this land to be now well worth 10s an acre....

v. *Clover*

Source: ibid. pp. 130–1

... The second grand point of Mr Turner's husbandry, has been
the introduction of clover. The farmers throughout Cleveland,
have, to this day, rejected the use of that noble vegetable; notwithstanding their possessing a fine rich clay soil, which reason tells one,
would produce vast crops of it. This gentleman has introduced the
use of it with the same spirit he exerts in all his views. He has sown
it upon large tracts of land, and with great success. One experiment,
in which he was accurate, is highly worthy of insertion.

A field, containing 13 acres of clover, and three acres in a
border of very bad natural grass, was sown with clover, among the
crop of last year: this year it has flourished greatly, and yielded the
following produce.

From Ladyday to the middle of May it kept 80 sheep and six young cattle. At old Midsummer it was mown for hay, of which it yielded as much as was worth £20 at the stack. After this it maintained 100 sheep and 20 oxen, two months; 16 cart horses, three weeks; two mares and two foals, a fortnight; and 60 sheep, six weeks. . . .

vi. *Cabbages*

Source: *ibid.* pp. 117–18, 126–7

. . . Cabbages, Mr Turner has cultivated from the year 1764, when he began his trials. That year he planted a rood and a half, upon a piece of ground that had been full of trees, which were stubbed. After this, it was ploughed in winter two or three times, and in the beginning of May planted in rows three feet asunder, the plants two feet from each other. They were only hand hoed, but the operation repeated three or four times: they were first used at Candlemas, for some fat oxen, and they eat them very heartily. They were the Scotch cabbage. The experiment, though not conclusive, gave great hope of success on a larger scale.

In 1765, two acres, a good loamy soil, were planted. An oat stubble was fixed upon in the preceding autumn, and fallowed for the purpose. The seed was sown in March. The 18th and 19th of June they were planted directly out of the seed-bed, in rows the same distance as before. They were horse-hoed twice with a common plough, and the rows hand-hoed as often. This crop was used between Christmas and Candlemas, and chiefly in a deep snow. Eighteen oxen were fatting on turnips, which being buried by the snow, the beasts were put to cabbages; they all ate them much better than the turnips.

A particular trial was made, by burying some cabbages in their feeding-trough under a heap of turnips; they turned aside the turnips at once, without biting one, and seized the cabbages with the utmost greediness. These two acres were part of twelve; the other ten sown with turnips. In the spring following the whole field was sown with barley: the part after the cabbages was much freer from weeds than the rest of the field, and yielded eight bushels per acre more than the rest of the field. This experiment, upon the whole, was very satisfactory; and the greatest motive for pursuing the culture with spirit. . . .

Besides cabbages, Mr Turner, this year, has two acres of brocoli upon a clay soil, planted at Midsummer, in rows of three feet asunder, the plants two feet from each other; they have been twice horse-hoed, and once hand-weeded. The design of using them was not in expectation of a great weight, but a food for sheep in the spring, the two last weeks in April. As this is the first experiment, the result is uncertain. . . .

vii. *Turnips for cattle*

Source: D. Defoe, *A Tour Through the Whole Island of Great Britain* (1726) I. i. p. 87

. . . This part of England [Suffolk] is also remarkable for being the first where the feeding and fattening of cattle, both sheep as well as black cattle with turnips, was first practised in England, which is made a very great part of the improvement of their lands to this day; and from whence the practice is spread over most of the east and south parts of England, to the great enriching of the farmers, and increase of fat cattle. And though some have objected against the goodness of the flesh thus fed with turnips, and have fancied it would taste of the root; yet upon experience 'tis found, that at market there is no difference nor can they that buy, single out one joint of mutton from another by the taste. So that the complaint which our nice palates at first made, begins to cease of itself; and a very great quantity of beef, and mutton also, is brought every year, and every week to London, from this side of England, and much more than was formerly known to be fed there. . . .

viii. *Cattle*

Source: A. Young, *A Six Months' Tour through the North of England* (1770) ii. pp. 133–5

. . . The third object of Mr Turner's economics, has been the improvement of the breed of cattle. Cleveland, though abounding with kinds which are good on comparison with several counties, yet did not the breed satisfy this gentleman, while better were to be had. An emulation, if I may so express it, highly laudable.

The breed of horned cattle common in this country is the short horned kind, called the Holderness breed improperly; but really the Dutch sort. These cattle are good for fatting, as they grow to a great weight, but for milking Mr Turner reckons them much inferior to the Lancashire short horned breed; and in fatting he likewise finds them in proportion to their weight easier fed, and more profitable. . . .

. . . Mr Turner did not procure a dairy of the true Lancashire long horned cows, without much trouble and great expense; for the great repute that breed has been in of late years, among the capital breeders of stock, has made the genuine breed sought after, and the pedigrees searched into, almost with as much attention as those of race horses. His first bull cost him 40 guineas; and he at the same time bought 15 cows, that cost him 20 guineas each; and to show the value of this breed for the purpose of breeding bulls it may not be amiss to remark, that Mr Turner was offered 60 guineas for two of these cows by the most famous stock-breeder perhaps in England, Mr Bakewell of Ditchley, near Loughborough in Leicestershire. . . .

❖

Trade and Industry

I. TEXTILES

i. *The South West*

The movement of the woollen industry to the West Riding had not yet affected the traditional centres.

i. *Source:* D. Defoe, *A Tour Through the Whole Island of Great Britain* (1726) II. ii. p. 44

1. We may reasonably conclude, that this manufacture was at first seated in this county [Wiltshire], or, as we may say, planted

itself here at first, because of the infinite numbers of sheep, which were fed at that time upon the downs and plains of Dorset, Wilts, and Hampshire, all adjoining, as a trading town is seated, or rises gradually upon some large river, because of the benefit of navigation; and as gentlemen place the mansion houses of their estates, and seats of their families, as near the pleasant rivers, woods, and fine prospects as possible, for the delight of their living; so the first planters of the clothing manufacture doubtless, chose this delightful vale for its seat, because of the neighbourhood of those plains, which might be supposed to be a fund of wool for the carrying it on. Thus the manufacture of white cloth was planted in Stroud Water in Gloucestershire, for the sake of the excellent water there for the dying scarlets, and all colours that are dyed in grain, which are better dyed there, than in any other place of England, some towns near London excepted. Hence, therefore, we first observe, they are supplied yearly with the fleeces of two or three millions of sheep.

2. But as the number of sheep fed on these downs is lessened, rather than increased, because of the many thousand acres of the carpet ground being, of late years, turned into arable land, and sowed with wheat; which, by the way, has made Warminster a market town, on the edge of Somersetshire, as it now is, without exception, the greatest market for wheat in England, with this exception only, viz. where none of it is bought to send to London.

I say, the number of sheep, and consequently the quantity of wool, decreasing, and at the same time the manufacture, as has been said, prodigiously increasing, the manufacturers applied themselves to other parts for a supply, and hence began the influx of north-country wool to come in from the counties of Northampton, Leicester, and Lincoln, the centre of which trade, is about Tetbury and Cirencester, where are the markets for the north-country wool, and where, as they say, several hundred packs of wool are sold every week, for the supply of this prodigious consumption.

3. From London, they have great quantities of wool, which is generally called Kentish wool, in the fleece, which is brought up from thence by the farmers, since the late severe Acts against their selling it within a certain number of miles of the sea, also fell-wool

for the combers, bought of the wool-staplers in Barnaby street, and sent back by the carriers, which bring up the cloths to market.

4. They have also, sometimes, large quantities of Irish wool, by the way of Bristol, or of Minehead, in Somersetshire; but this is uncertain, and only on extraordinary occasions. I omit the Spanish wool, as being an article by itself. . . .

ii. *Source: ibid.* II. ii. p. 41

. . . These towns [in Wiltshire] as they stand thin, and at considerable distance from one another; for except the two towns of Bradford and Trowbridge, the others stand at an unusual distance; I say, these towns are interspersed with a very great number of villages, I had almost said, innumerable villages, hamlets, and scattered houses, in which, generally speaking, the spinning work of all this manufacture is performed by the poor people; the master clothiers, who generally live in the greater towns, sending out the wool weekly to their houses, by their servants and horses, and, at the same time, bringing back the yarn that they have spun and finished, which then is fitted for the loom.

ii. *East Anglia*
Source: ibid. I. i. p. 92

. . . An eminent weaver of Norwich gave me a scheme of their trade on this occasion, by which, calculating from the number of looms at that time employed in the city of Norwich only, besides those employed in other towns in the same county, he made it appear very plain, that there were 120,000 people employed in the woollen and silk and wool manufactures of that city only, not that the people all lived in the city, tho' Norwich is a very large and populous city too. But I say, they were employed for spinning the yarn used for such goods as were all made in that city. . . .

This shows the wonderful extent of the Norwich manufacture, or stuff-weaving trade, by which so many thousands of families are maintained. Their trade indeed felt a very sensible decay, and the cries of the poor began to be very loud, when the wearing of painted calicoes was grown to such an height in England, as was seen about two or three years ago; but an Act of Parliament having been obtained, though not without great struggle, in the years 1720, and 1721, for prohibiting the use and wearing of calicoes, the stuff trade revived incredibly; and as I passed this part of the country in the year 1723, the manufacturers assured me that there was not in all the eastern and middle part of Norfolk any hand, unemployed, if they would work; and that the very children after four or five years of age, could every one earn their own bread. . . .

iii. *The West Riding Cloth Industry*

   i. *Source:* A. Young, *A Six Months' Tour through the North of England* (1770) i. pp. 151–3

   . . . At this town [Leeds], but more in the neighbourhood, is carried on a vast manufacturing trade: Leeds cloth market is well known, and has been often described. They make chiefly broad cloths from 1s 8d a yard, to 12s but mostly of 4s 6d and 5s. Good hands at this branch, would earn about 10s 6d a week, the year round if they were fully employed; but as it is, cannot make above 8s. This difference of 2s 6d is a melancholy consideration. A boy of 13 or 14, about 4s a week, some women earn by weaving as much as the men. The men, at what they call offal work, which is the inferior branches, such as picking, printing, etc. are paid 1d an hour. Besides broad cloths, there are some shalloons,[1] and many stuffs made at Leeds, particularly Scotch camblets,[2] grograms,[3] burdies,[4] some calimancoes,[5] etc. The weavers earn from 5s to 12s a week; upon an average 7s. Boys of 13 or 14, 5s a week. But they are all thrown out in bad weather; men in general at an average the year round, about 6s or 6s 6d a week. They never want work at weaving. Dressers earn from 1s to 3s a day, but are much thrown out by want of work. The women by weaving stuffs, earn 3s 6d or 4s a week. Wool combers, 6s to 12s a week. The spinning trade

[1] Woollen material used for dresses and linings.
[2] A mixed cloth.
[3] Coarse fabric of silk.
[4] A cotton fabric.
[5] A mixture of wool and satin in a chequered pattern.

is constant, women earn about 2s 6d or 3s a week. Girls of 13 or 14 earn 1s 8d a week. A boy of 8 or 9 at ditto, 2½d a day; of six year old, 1d a day. . . .

ii. *Source:* D. Defoe, *A Tour Through the Whole Island of Great Britain* (1726) III. pp. 97–101

This business [in Halifax] is the clothing trade, for the convenience of which the houses are thus scattered and spread upon the sides of the hills, as above, even from the bottom to the top; the reason is this: such has been the bounty of nature to this otherwise frightful country, that two things essential to the business, as well as to the ease of the people are found here, and that in a situation which I never saw the like of in any part of England; and, I believe, the like is not to be seen so contrived in any part of the world; I mean coals and running water upon the tops of the highest hills. This seems to have been directed by the wise hand of Providence for the very purpose which is now served by it, namely, the manufactures, which otherwise could not be carried on; neither indeed could one fifth part of the inhabitants be supported without them, for the land could not maintain them. After we had mounted the third hill, we found the country, in short, one continued village, though mountainous every way, as before; hardly a house standing out of a speaking distance from another, and (which soon told us their business) the day clearing up, and the sun shining, we could see that almost at every house there was a tenter,[1] and almost on every tenter a piece of cloth, or kersie, or shalloon, for they are the three articles of that country's labour. . . .

But to return to the reason of dispersing the houses, as above; I found, as our road passed among them, for indeed no road could do otherwise, wherever we passed any house we found a little rill or gutter of running water; if the house was above the road, it came from it, and crossed the way to run to another; if the house was below us, it crossed us from some other distant house above it, and at every considerable house was a manufactury or work-house, and as they could not do their business without water, the little streams were so parted and guided by gutters or pipes, and by

[1] Machine for stretching cloth.

turning and dividing the streams, that none of those houses were without a river, if I may call it so, running into and through their work-houses.

Again, as the dying-houses, scouring-shops, and places where they used this water, emitted the water again, ting'd with the drugs of the dying fat, and with the oil, the soap, the tallow, and other ingredients used by the clothiers in dressing and scouring, etc. which then runs away through the lands to the next, the grounds are not only universally watered, how dry soever the season, but that water so ting'd and so fattened enriches the lands they run through that 'tis hardly to be imagined how fertile and rich the soil is made by it. . . .

2. COAL AND IRON

i. *Source:* A. Young, *A Six Months' Tour through the North of England* (1770) iii. pp. 12–14

. . . The people employed in the coal-mines are prodigiously numerous, amounting to many thousands; the earnings of the men are from 1s to 4s a day, and their firing. The coal waggon roads, from the pits to the water, are great works, carried over all sorts of inequalities of ground, so far as the distance of 9 or 10 miles. The tracks of the wheels are marked with pieces of timber let into the road, for the wheels of the waggons to run on, by which means one horse is enabled to draw, and that with ease, 50 or 60 bushels of coals. There are many other branches of business that have much carriage in a regular track, that greatly wants this improvement, which tends so considerably to the lowering the expenses of carriage.

About five miles from Newcastle are the iron works, late Crawleys', supposed to be the greatest manufactory of the kind in Europe. Several hundred hands are employed in it, insomuch that £20,000 a year is paid in wages. They earn from 1s to 2s 6d a day; and some of the foremen so high as £200 a year. The quantity of iron they work up is very great, employing three ships to the Baltic, that each make ten voyages yearly, and bring 70 tons at a time, which amounts to 2,100 tons, besides 500 tons more freighted in others. They use a good deal of American iron, which is as good as any Swedish, and for some purposes much better. . . .

They use annually 7,000 bolls[1] of coals, at 16 bushels each.

They manufacture anchors as high as 70 cwt., carriages of cannon, hoes, spades, axes, hooks, chains, etc. etc.

In general their greatest work is for exportation, and [they] are employed very considerably by the East India Company. They have of late had a prodigious artillery demand from that Company.

During the war their business was extremely great. It was worse upon the peace; but for anchors and mooring chains the demand these last 7 or 8 years has been very regular and spirited. . . .

ii. *Source:* D. Defoe, *A Tour through the Whole Island of Great Britain* (1726) III. p. 191

. . . From hence [Lumley, near Durham] the road to Newcastle gives a view of the inexhausted store of coals and coal pits, from whence not London only, but all the south part of England is continually supplied; and whereas when we are at London, and see the prodigious fleets of ships which come constantly in with coals for this increasing city, we are apt to wonder whence they come, and, that they do not bring the whole country away; so, on the contrary, when in this country we see the prodigious heaps, I might say mountains, of coals, which are dug up at every pit, and how many of those pits there are; we are filled with equal wonder to consider where the people should live that can consume them. . . .

iii. In the early eighteenth century the iron industry was still centred in the traditional area of the Weald.

Source: ibid. I. ii. p. 106

. . . All this part of the country is very agreeably pleasant, wholesome and fruitful, I mean quite from Guildford to this place [Westerham in Kent], and is accordingly overspread with good

[1] A boll is equal to 140 lb.

towns, gentlemen's houses, populous villages, abundance of fruit, with hop-grounds and cherry orchards, and the lands well cultivated; but all on the right-hand, that is to say, south, is exceedingly grown with timber, has abundance of waste, and wild grounds, and forests, and woods, with many large iron-works, at which they cast great quantities of iron caldrons, chimney-backs, furnaces, retorts, boiling pots, and all such necessary things of iron; besides iron cannon, bomb-shells, stink-pots,[1] hand-grenadoes, and cannon ball, etc., in an infinite quantity, and which turn to very great account; tho' at the same time the works are prodigiously expensive, and the quantity of wood they consume is exceeding great, which keeps up that complaint I mentioned before; that timber would grow scarce, and consequently dear, from the great quantity consumed in the iron-works in Sussex. . . .

3. TRADE

i. *Source:* D. Defoe, *A Tour through the Whole Island of Great Britain* (1726) I. i. p. 62

. . . But the neighbourhood of London, which sucks the vitals of trade in this island to itself, is the chief reason of any decay of business in this place [Ipswich], and I shall in the course of these observations, hint at it, where many good sea-ports and large towns, though farther off than Ipswich, and as well fitted for commerce, are yet swallowed up by the immense indraft of trade to the city of London; and more decayed beyond all comparison, than Ipswich is supposed to be; as Southampton, Weymouth, Dartmouth, and several others which I shall speak to in their order. And if it be otherwise at this time, with some other towns, which are lately increased in trade and navigation, wealth, and people, while their neighbours decay, it is because they have some particular trade or accident to trade, which is a kind of nostrum to them, inseparable to the place, and which fixes there by the nature of the thing; as the herring-fishery to Yarmouth; the coal trade to Newcastle;

---

[1] A hand missile giving off suffocating smoke.

the Leeds clothing-trade; the export of butter and lead, and the great corn trade for Holland, is to Hull; the Virginia and West-India trade at Liverpool, the Irish trade at Bristol, and the like. Thus the war has brought a flux of business and people, and consequently of wealth, to several places, as well as to Portsmouth, Chatham, Plymouth, Falmouth, and others; and were any wars like those, to continue 20 years with the Dutch, or any nation whose fleets lay that way, as the Dutch do, it would be the like perhaps at Ipswich in a few years, and at other places on the same coast.

ii. *Source: ibid.* I. i. p. 100

... The quantity of herrings that are catched in this season are diversely accounted for; some have said, that the towns of Yarmouth and Lowestoft only, have taken forty thousand last[1] in a season; I will not venture to confirm that report; but this I have heard the merchants themselves say, (viz) That they have cured, that is to say, hanged and dried in the smoke, 40,000 barrels of merchantable redherrings in one season, which is in itself (though far short of the other) yet a very considerable article; and it is to be added, that this is besides all the herrings consumed in the country towns of both those populous counties, for thirty miles from the sea, whither very great quantities are carried every tide during the whole season.

But this is only one branch of the great trade carried on in this town [Yarmouth]. Another part of this commerce, is in the exporting these herrings after they are cured; and for this their merchants have a great trade to Genoa, Leghorn, Naples, Messina, and Venice; as also to Spain and Portugal, also exporting with their herring very great quantities of worsted stuffs, and stuffs made of silk and worsted, camblets,[2] &c. the manufactures of the neighbouring city of Norwich, and the places adjacent.

Besides this, they carry on a very considerable trade with Holland, whose opposite neighbours they are; and a vast quantity of woollen manufactures they export to the Dutch every year.

[1] A last is twelve barrels.
[2] A mixed cloth.

171

Also they have a fishing trade to the north-seas for white fish, which from the place are called the North-Sea cod.

They have also a considerable trade to Norway, and to the Baltic, from whence they bring back deals, and fir-timber, oaken plank, baulks, spars, oars, pitch, tar, hemp, flax, spruce, canvas, and sail-cloth; with all manner of naval stores, which they generally have a consumption for in their own part, where they build a very great number of ships every year, besides re-fitting and repairing the old.

Add to this the coal trade between Newcastle and the river of Thames, in which they are so improved of late years, that they have now a greater share of it than any other town in England; and have quite worked the Ipswich men out of it, who had formerly the chief share of the colliery in their hands. . . .

iii. *Colonial Rivalry in the West Indies*

Despite the Navigation Acts, which were obviously not being enforced, foreign trade in the West Indies was rapidly developing.

Source: C.S.P. America and West Indies (1730) p. 359

Petition of the Planters, Traders and other inhabitants of Barbados to the King. This your Island of Barbados was the first settled and mother of all your Majesty's Sugar Colonies and has for many years past been a very profitable Colony to Great Britain not only from its produce and import of sugar, rum, molasses, cotton, ginger and alloes into Great Britain, the taking off from thence great quantities of woollen and other manufactures and goods that pay duties to the Crown (which by means of the Barbados trade are not only consumed among the inhabitants here but are also exported from Great Britain to Africa, Madeira, and the Northern Colonies for the purchase of negroes, wine, fish and other goods for the use of this island and thereby numberless hands have been employed in your Majesty's Kingdoms and Territories and great revenues have accrued and do still continually accrue to the Crown) but has also been a great support to your Majesty's Northern Colonies and given a very great and profitable vent to their Fishery and other produce and also to the produce of Ireland, besides employing in those several trades great numbers of shipping and seamen on which the wealth and safety of the British Nation does so much depend, and after all leaves a considerable balance in England to the benefit of the national stock. Within these few years great improvements have been made by the Dutch and French in their Sugar Colonies and great and extraordinary encouragements have been given to them not only from their mother countries but also from a pernicious trade carried on by them to and from Ireland and the Northern British Colonies, and the French do now from the produce of their own Sugar Colonies actually supply with sugar not only France itself but Spain, also a great part of Ireland and the British Northern Colonies, and have to spare for Holland, Germany, Italy and other parts of Europe, and the French and Dutch Colonies have lately supplied the Northern British Colonies with very large quantities of molasses for the making of rum and other uses, and even with rum of their own manufacture to the vast prejudice of your Majesty's Sugar Colonies as rum is a commodity on which next to sugar they most depend . . . Your Majesty's subjects of your Sugar Colonies have already suffered very much and must inevitably be undone thereby unless your Majesty will in your great goodness interpose and save them from the ruin now impending over them, which your Petitioners humbly conceive may be effected if order be taken to prevent any sugar, rum or molasses of the growth, produce and manufacture of foreign Plantations from being imported into Ireland or any of the British Plantations or Colonies in America until they have been first imported into Great Britain and paid such duties there to your Majesty as those commodities are now liable to, or that your Majesty's subjects of your Sugar Colonies may have the like advantages in these branches of commerce as the subjects of Foreign Powers now actually have.

Education

An Eighteenth Century View

Source: B. Mandeville, 'An Essay on Charity and Charity Schools' in *The Fable of the Bees* (1732) p. 328

Plate 28(a)

. . . It is manifest that in a free nation where slaves are not allowed, the surest wealth consists in a multitude of laborious poor; for besides that they are the never failing nursery of fleets and armies, without them there could be no enjoyment and no product of any country could be valuable. To make society happy and people easy under the meanest circumstances, it is requisite that great numbers of them should be ignorant as well as poor. Knowledge both enlarges and multiplies our desires, and the fewer things a man wishes for, the more easily his necessities may be supplied.

The welfare and felicity therefore of every state and kingdom, require that the knowledge of the working poor should be confined within the verge of their occupations, and never extended (as to things visible) beyond what relates to their calling. The more a shepherd, a ploughman, or any other peasant knows of the world, and the things that are foreign to his labour or employment, the less fit he'll be to go through the fatigues and hardships of it with cheerfulness and content.

Reading, writing, and arithmetic are very necessary to those whose business require such qualifications, but where people's livelihood has no dependence on those arts, they are very pernicious to the poor, who are forced to get their daily bread by their daily labour. Few children make any progress at school, but at the same time they are capable of being employed in some business or other, so that every hour those of poor people spend at their book is so much time lost to society. Going to school in comparison to working is idleness, and the longer boys continue in this easy sort of life, the more unfit they'll be when grown up for downright labour, both as to strength and inclination. Men who are to remain and end their days in a laborious, tiresome and painful station of life, the sooner they are put upon it at first, the more patiently they'll submit to it for ever after. Hard labour and the coarsest diet is a proper punishment to several kinds of malefactors, but to impose either on those that have not been brought up to both is the greatest cruelty, when there is no crime that you can charge them with. . . . Those who spent a great part of their youth in learning to read, write, and cypher expect, and not unjustly, to be employed where those qualifications may be of use to them; the generality of them will look upon downright labour with the utmost contempt. A man who has had some education, may follow husbandry by choice, and may be diligent at the dirtiest and most laborious work; but then the concern must be his own, and avarice, the care of a family, or some other pressing motive must put him upon it, but he won't make a good hireling and serve a farmer for a pitiful reward, at least he is not so fit for it as a day labourer that has always been employed about the plough and dung-cart, and remembers not that ever he has lived otherwise.

❖

Roads

i. State of the Roads

Source: D. Defoe, *A Tour through the Whole Island of Great Britain* (1726) I. ii. p. 60; II. i. p. 185

i. . . . Sometimes a whole summer is not dry enough to make the roads passable: here I had a sight, which indeed I never saw in any other part of England: namely, that going to church at a country village, not far from Lewes, I saw an ancient lady, and a lady of very good quality, I assure you, drawn to church in her coach with six oxen; nor was it done in frolic or humour, but mere necessity, the way being so stiff and deep, that no horses could go in it.

ii. . . . Here [in Hertfordshire] is that famous lane call'd Baldock Lane, famous for being so unpassable, that the coaches and travellers were oblig'd to break out of the way even by force, which the people of the country not able to prevent, at length placed gates, and laid their lands open, setting men at the gates to take a voluntary toll, which travellers always chose to pay, rather than plunge into sloughs and holes, which no horse could wade through.

ii. *Turnpikes*

i. *Source: ibid.* II. i. p. 183

Plate 28

. . . These roads [in Essex] were formerly deep, in time of floods dangerous, and at other times, in winter, scarce passable; they are now so firm, so safe, so easy to travellers, and carriages as well as cattle, that no road in England can yet be said to equal them; this was first done by the help of a turnpike, set up by Act of Parliament, about the year 1697, at a village near Ingerstone. Since that, another turnpike, set up at the corner of the Dog Row, near Mile-end; with an additional one at Rumford, which is called a branch, and paying at one, passes the person thro' both. This I say, being set up since the other, completes the whole, and we are told, that as the first expires in a year or two, this last will be sufficient for the whole, which will be a great ease to the country. The first toll near Ingerstone, being the highest rated public toll in England; for they take 8d for every cart, 6d for every coach, and 12d for every wagon; and in proportion for droves of cattle. For single horsemen indeed, it is the same as others pay, viz. 1d per horse, and we are told, while this is doing, that the gentlemen of the county design to petition the Parliament, to have the Commissioners of the last Act, whose turnpike, as above, is at Mile-end and Rumford empowered to take other turnpikes, on the other most considerable roads, and so to undertake, and repair all the roads in the whole county, I mean all the considerable roads.

iii. Stage-coaches

Source: C. Moritz, *Travels in England in 1782* (1795) pp. 112, 246
Plate 26

... I must observe, that they have here a curious way of riding, not in, but upon, a stage-coach. Persons, to whom it is not convenient to pay a full price, instead of the inside, sit on the top of the coach, without any seats, or even a rail. By what means passengers thus fasten themselves securely on the roof of these vehicles, I know not; but you constantly see numbers seated there, apparently at their ease, and in perfect safety.

This they call riding on the outside; for which they pay only half as much as those pay, who are within: we had at present six of these passengers over our heads, who, when we alighted, frequently made such a noise, and bustle, as sometimes almost frightened us. He who can properly balance himself, rides not incommodiously on the outside; and in summer time, in fine weather, on account of the prospects, it certainly is more pleasant than it is within; excepting that the company is generally low, and the dust is likewise more troublesome than in the inside, where, at any rate, you may draw up the windows according to your pleasure.

... But this ride from Leicester to Northampton, I shall remember as long as I live.

The coach drove from the yard through a part of the house. The inside passengers got in, in the yard; but we on the outside were obliged to clamber up in the public street, because we should have had no room for our heads to pass under the gateway.

My companions on the top of the coach, were a farmer, a young man very decently dressed, and a black-a-moor.

The getting up along was at the risk of one's life; and when I was up, I was obliged to sit just at the corner of the coach, with nothing to hold by, but a sort of little handle fastened on the side. I sat nearest the wheel; and the moment that we set off, I fancied that I saw certain death await me. All I could do, was to take still faster hold of the handle, and to be more and more careful to preserve my balance.

The machine now rolled along with prodigious rapidity, over the stones through the town, and every moment we seemed to fly into the air; so that it was almost a miracle, that we still stuck to the coach, and did not fall. We seemed to be thus on the wing, and to fly, as often as we passed through a village, or went down an hill.

At last the being continually in fear of my life, became insupportable, and as we were going up a hill, and consequently proceeding rather slower than usual, I crept from the top of the coach, and got snug into the basket.

'O, sir, sir, you will be shaken to death!' said the black; but I flattered myself, he exaggerated the unpleasantness of my post.

As long as we went up hill, it was easy and pleasant. And, having had little or no sleep the night before, I was almost asleep among the trunks and the packages; but how was the case altered when we came to go down hill; then all the trunks and parcels began, as it were, to dance around me, and every thing in the basket seemed to be alive; and I every moment received from them such violent blows, that I thought my last hour was come. I now found that what the black had told me, was no exaggeration; but all my complaints were useless. I was obliged to suffer this torture nearly an hour, till we came to another hill again, when quite shaken to pieces and sadly bruised, I again crept to the top of the coach, and took possession of my former seat. 'Ah, did not I tell you that you would be shaken to death?' said the black, as I was getting up; but I made him no reply. Indeed I was ashamed; and I now write this as a warning to all strangers to stage-coaches who may happen to take it into their heads, without being used to it, to take a place on the outside of an English post-coach; and still more, a place in the basket.

iv. *Highwaymen*

Source: H. Walpole, *Letters* (ed. P. Cunningham, 1857–9) viii. p. 88

To the Countess of Ossory

Strawberry Hill, October 7, 1781

The night I had the honour of writing to your Ladyship last, I was robbed . . . *Voici le fait.* Lady Browne and I were, as usual, going to the Duchess of Montrose at seven o'clock. The evening was very dark. In the close lane under her park-pale, and within twenty yards of the gate, a black figure on horseback pushed by between the chaise and the hedge on my side. I suspected it was a highwayman, and so I found did Lady Browne, for she was speaking and stopped. To divert her fears, I was just going to say, 'Is not that the apothecary going to the Duchess?' when I heard a voice cry, 'Stop!' and the figure came back to the chaise.

I had the presence of mind, before I let down the glass, to take out my watch and stuff it within my waistcoat under my arm. He said, 'Your purses and watches!' I replied, 'I have no watch.' 'Then your purse!' I gave it to him; it had nine guineas. It was so dark that I could not see his hand, but felt him take it. He then asked for Lady Browne's purse, and said, 'Don't be frightened; I will not hurt you.' I said, 'No; you won't frighten the lady?' He replied, 'No; I give you my word I will do you no hurt.' Lady Browne gave him her purse, and was going to add her watch, but he said, 'I am much obliged to you! I wish you goodnight!' pulled off his hat, and rode away.

'Well,' said I, 'Lady Browne, you will not be afraid of being robbed another time, for you see there is nothing in it.' 'Oh! but I am,' said she, 'and now I am in terrors lest he should return, for I have given him a purse with only bad money that I carry on purpose.' 'He certainly will not open it directly,' said I, 'and at the worst he can only wait for us at our return; but I will send my servant back for a horse and a blunderbuss,' which I did. . . .

v. *John Metcalf, Blind Jack of Knaresborough* (1717–1810)
   Source: S. Smiles, *Lives of Engineers* (1862) i. p. 225

One who personally knew Metcalf thus wrote of him during his lifetime: with the assistance only of a long staff, I have several times met this man traversing the roads, ascending steep and rugged heights, exploring valleys and investigating their several extents, forms, and situations, so as to answer his designs in the best manner. The plans which he makes, and the estimate he prepares, are done in a method peculiar to himself, and of which he cannot well convey the meaning to others. His abilities in this respect are, nevertheless, so great that he finds constant employment. Most of the roads over the Peak in Derbyshire have been altered by his directions, particularly those in the vicinity of Buxton; and he is at this time constructing a new one betwixt Wilmslow and Congleton, to open a communication with the great London road without being obliged to pass over the mountains. I have met this blind projector while engaged in making his survey. He was alone as usual, and amongst other conversation, I have made some enquiries respecting this new road. It was really astonishing to hear with what accuracy he described its course and the nature of the different soils through which it was conducted. Having mentioned to him a boggy piece of ground it passed through, he observed that that was the only place he had doubts concerning, and he was apprehensive they had, contrary to his directions, been too sparing of their materials.

❖

Transport in London

i. *Source:* C. de Saussure, *A Foreign View of England in the Reigns of George I and George II* (1902) p. 165

The hackney-coaches in London are a great convenience. About one thousand of these vehicles are to be found day and night in the public places and principal streets of the city and town. Most of them, to tell the truth, are ugly and dirty. The driver is perched high up on a wooden seat, as elevated as the imperial[1] of a coach. The body of the carriage is very badly balanced, so that when inside you are most cruelly shaken, the pavement being very uneven, and most of the horses excellent and fast trotters. A drive costs one shilling, provided you do not go further than a certain distance; other drives will cost two or sometimes three shillings, according to distance. The drivers often ask more than is their

[1] The trunk for luggage on the roof.

due, and this is the case especially when they have to do with foreigners. To avoid being cheated, you must take the number of the coach marked on the door, and offer the driver a handful of coins, telling him to take his fare out of it. In this fashion of dealing he will not take more than his due, for should he do so you have a right to go and complain at the coach office, and the driver will be punished by being made to pay a fine, half of which would go to the plaintiff, and the other half to the officers of the office.

Besides these conveyances there are a great number of chariots and coaches belonging to noblemen and to gentlemen. Some are magnificent, and most are drawn by fine and excellent horses. The chariots belonging to noblemen are recognizable by the small gilt coronets placed at each of the four corners of the imperial; those belonging to dukes have ducal coronets and so on. These fine chariots, behind which stand two or three footmen attired in rich liveries, are certainly a great ornament to town, and a convenience to rich people, but they are a great hindrance to those who are not wealthy and go on foot, for the streets being generally very muddy, the passers-by get terribly bespattered and dirty. Pedestrians, it is true, would be far worse off were there not on either side of the street a sort of elevated foot-path for their convenience, but I think I have already told you of this.

Near the palace and in its vicinity there are more than three hundred sedan-chairs for hire; like the cabs, they are found in the principal streets and thoroughfares. Chairs are very convenient and pleasant for use, the bearers going so fast that you have some difficulty in keeping up with them on foot. I do not believe that in the whole of Europe better or more dexterous bearers are to be found; all foreigners are surprised at their strength and skill. Like coaches, sedan-chairs are most convenient for the wealthy, but often very embarrassing for those of another class, for these chairs are allowed to be carried on the foot-paths, and when a person does not take heed, or a stranger does not understand the 'Have care', or 'By your leave, sir', of the bearers and does not make room to let them pass, he will run a great risk of being knocked down, for the bearers go very fast and cannot turn aside with their burden.

I went through this experience on first coming to London. Not understanding the 'By your leave', addressed to me, I did not draw aside, and repented quickly, for I received a tremendous push which hurled me four feet further on, and I should undoubtedly have fallen on my back had it not been for the wall of a house which broke my fall, but much to the injury of my arm. To my cost I thus learnt what the cry of the bearer means. Sedan-chairs are also numbered and there is an office where you can go and make your complaint if cheated by your bearers.

ii. *Source:* M. Misson, *Memoirs and Observations* (1719) p. 21

The little boats upon the Thames, which are only for carrying of persons, are light and pretty; some are rowed by one man, others by two. The former are called scullers and the latter oars. They are reckoned at several thousands, but though there are indeed a great many, I believe the number is exaggerated. The city of London being very long, it is a great conveniency to be able sometimes to make use of this way of carriage. You sit at your ease upon cushions and have a board to lean against, but generally they have no covering, unless a cloth which the watermen set up immediately, in case of need, over a few hoops, and sometimes you are wet to the skin for all this. It is easy to conceive that the oars go faster than the sculls and accordingly their pay is doubled. You never have no disputes [*sic*] with them, for you can go to no part either of London or the country, above or below it, but the rate is fixed by authority, everything is regulated and printed. The same is done with respect to hackney-coaches and carts for the carriage of goods.

❖

Canals

Source: A. Young, *A Six Months' Tour through the North of England* (1770) iii. pp. 251, 266

Plate 29

The original design of the Duke of Bridgwater, was to cut a canal from Worsley, an estate of his Grace's, abounding with coal-mines, to Manchester, for the easy conveyance of his coals to so considerable a market; and, in 1758–9, an Act of Parliament for that purpose was obtained. The course of the canal prescribed by this Act, was afterwards varied by the same authority, and the Duke further enabled greatly to extend his plan; for he now determined, and with uncommon spirit, to make his canal branch not only from Worsley to Manchester, but also from a part of the canal between both, to Stockport and Liverpool. The idea was a noble one, and ranks this spirited young nobleman with the most useful genius's of this or any age. But the execution of so great a plan teemed with difficulties that required a perpetual exertion of abilities fertile in resources. . . .

[One of the major difficulties was solved by Brindley's Barton Aqueduct—see Plate 29]

. . . The effect of coming at once on to Barton Bridge, and looking down upon a large river, with barges of great burthen sailing on it; and up to another river, hung in the air, with barges towing along it, form altogether a scenery somewhat like enchantment, and exhibit at once a view that must give you an idea of prodigious labour; for the canal is here not only carried over the Irwell, but likewise across a large valley, being banked up on each side in a surprising manner, to form a mound for the water, and the channel also filled up to the usual depth, that the banks, at a place where they are entirely artificial, and consequently weaker than where natural, might not be endangered by the great pressure of so large a body of water as the depth here filled up would have contained: and I should remark that it is a maxim throughout this whole navigation, to keep the canal of an equal depth everywhere: I believe it scarce ever varies above six inches; from four feet, to four feet six inches. . . .

The Evil of Gin-Drinking

Source: Taken from an eighteenth-century print of Hogarth's *Gin Lane* in the Department of Prints and Drawings, British Museum

Plate 20

Gin, cursed fiend! with fury fraught,
Makes human race a prey;
It enters by a deadly draught,
And steals our life away.

Virtue and truth, driv'n to despair,
Its rage compels to fly,
But cherishes with hellish care,
Theft, murder, perjury.

Damn'd cup! That on the vitals preys,
That liquid fire contains;
Which madness to the heart conveys,
And rolls it thro' the veins.

This abominable liquor is, among the vulgar, very justly called by the name of 'Strip-me-naked'.

❖

Coffee Houses

Source: J. Macky, *Journey Through England* (1724) i. p. 107

Plate 17

. . . I am lodged in the street called Pall-Mall, the ordinary residence of all strangers, because of its vicinity to the King's

Palace, the Park, the Parliament House, the theatres, and the chocolate and coffee-houses, where the best company frequent. If you would know our manner of living it is thus: we rise by nine, and those that frequent great men's levées find entertainment at them till eleven; or, as in Holland, go to tea-tables. About twelve the *beau-monde* assembles in various chocolate and coffee-houses, the best of which are the Cocoa Tree and White's Chocolate-houses, St James's; the Smyrna and the British Coffee-houses and all these so near one another, that in less than an hour you see the company of them all. We are carried to these places in chairs [sedans], which are here very cheap, a guinea a week or a shilling per hour; and your chairmen serve you for porters to run on errands, as your gondoliers do at Venice.

If it be fine weather we take a turn in the park till two, when we go to dinner; and if it be dirty, you are entertained at picket or basset at White's, or you may talk politics at the Smyrna and St James's. I must not forget to tell you that the parties have their different places, where, however, a stranger is always well received; but a Whig will no more go to the Cocoa Tree or Ozinda's, than a Tory will be seen at the Coffee-house of St James's.

The Scots generally go to the British, and a mixture of all sorts to the Smyrna. There are other little coffee-houses much frequented in this neighbourhood—Youngman's, for officers; Oldman's for stockjobbers, paymasters and courtiers; and Little-man's for sharpers. I never was so confounded in my life as when I entered into this last; I saw two or three tables full at faro, heard the box and dice rattling in the room above stairs, and was surrounded by a set of sharp faces that I was afraid would have devoured me with their eyes. I was glad to drop two or three half-crowns at faro to get off with a clear skin, and was overjoyed I was so got rid of them.

At two we generally go to dinner. Ordinaries are not so common here as abroad, yet the French have set up two or three pretty good ones for the conveniency of foreigners, in Suffolk-street, where one is tolerably well served; but the general way here is to make a party at the coffee-house to go dine at the tavern, where we sit till six, then we go to the play.

After the play, the best company generally go to Tom's and

Willis's coffee-houses near adjoining, where there is playing at picket and the best of conversation till midnight. Here you will see blue and green ribands and stars sitting familiarly with private gentlemen, and talking with the same freedom as if they had left their quality and degrees of distance at home; and a stranger tastes with pleasure the universal liberty of speech of the English nation. Or if you like rather the company of ladies, there are assemblies at most people of quality's houses. And in all the coffee-houses you have not only the foreign prints, but several English ones, with the foreign occurrences, besides papers of morality and party disputes.

❖

Tea-Drinking Denounced

The habit of tea-drinking was spreading rapidly in the eighteenth century, but was regarded by some as both dangerous and wasteful.

Source: Jonas Hanway, *Letters on the Importance of the Rising Generation* (1867) ii. pp. 178–81

. . . It is sometimes difficult to determine what particular cause operates strongest in the decline of nations. But if we may judge from the nature of tea, and the universality of the fashion, the expense it creates to the poor, and the contraband trade it occasions, it will in the issue prove extremely hurtful to the nation.

. . . When it is genuine it hurts many, when adulterated or dyed, it has been found poisonous. The young and old, the healthy and infirm, the superlatively rich, down to vagabonds and beggars, drink this enchanting beverage, when they are thirsty and when they are not thirsty. Many kinds of tea are corrosive, and being made strong, is also an emetic, and as such often taken. . . .

. . . What a deplorable situation is that poor creature in, who having but three-pence or a groat a day, consumes a quarter part, or more, of her income in the infusion of a drug which is but a remove from poison. If six millions of pounds weight are consumed, deducting children under seven years old, it is above a pound each for a year, and at 7s charge on a medium is above 2 millions, near 4 per cent on our expense.

The ordinary charge of tea-drinking among the lowest part of the people is 1¼ penny a time. Considering the fuel they consume, and also the butter which frequently attends this entertainment, it must multiply wants and impoverish. Many who are crying out against wheat at 6s or 7s a bushel, will give up a pound of bread, rather than a quarter of an ounce of tea, or afternoon's amusement, in drinking this drug. Those who drink it twice a day, it will amount to near 2½ pence, which is more than a good dinner properly cooked will amount to.

❖

Inoculation against Small-Pox

Source: The Letters and Works of Lady Mary Wortley Montagu (1803) ii. p. 217

... A propos of distempers, I am going to tell you a thing that I am sure will make you wish yourself here. The small-pox, so fatal, and so general amongst us, is here [in Turkey] entirely harmless by the invention of ingrafting which is the term they give it. There is a set of old women who make it their business to perform the operation every autumn, in the month of September, when the great heat is abated. People send to one another to know if any of their family has a mind to have the small-pox: they make parties for this purpose, and when they are met (commonly fifteen or sixteen together), the old woman comes with a nutshell full of the matter of the best sort of small-pox and asks what veins you please to have opened. She immediately rips open that you offer to her with a large needle (which gives you no more pain than a common scratch), and puts into the vein as much venom as can lie upon the head of her needle, and after binds up the little wound with a hollow bit of shell; and in this manner opens four or five veins. The Grecians have commonly the superstition of opening one in the middle of the forehead, in each arm, and on the breast, to make the sign of the cross; but this has a very ill effect, all these wounds leaving little scars, and is not done by those that are not superstitious, who choose to have them in the legs, or that part of the arm that is concealed. The children or young patients play together all the rest of the day, and are in perfect health to the eighth. Then the fever begins to seize them, and they keep their beds two days, very seldom three. They have very rarely above twenty or thirty in their faces, which never mark; and in eight days' time they are as well as before their illness. Where they are wounded, there remain running sores during the distemper, which I don't doubt is a great relief to it. Every year thousands undergo this operation; and the French ambassador says pleasantly, that they take the small-pox here by way of diversion, as they take the waters in other countries. There is no example of any one that has died in it; and you may believe I am very well satisfied of the safety of this experiment, since I intend to try it on my dear little son.

I am patriot enough to take pains to bring this useful invention into fashion in England; and I should not fail to write to some of our doctors very particularly about it, if I knew any one of them that I thought had virtue enough to destroy such a considerable branch of their revenue for the good of mankind. But that distemper is too beneficial to them not to expose to all their resentment the hardy wight that should undertake to put an end to it. Perhaps, if I live to return, I may, however, have courage to war with them.

❖

The Manners of a Gentleman

Source: Lord Chesterfield, *Letters to his Son* (1774) i. p. 145

Spa. July 25, 1741

Dear Boy, I have often told you in my former letters (and it is most certainly true) that the strictest and most scrupulous honour and virtue can alone make you esteemed and valued by mankind;

that parts and learning can alone make you admired and celebrated by them; but that the possession of lesser talents was most absolutely necessary towards making you liked, beloved, and sought after in private life. Of these lesser talents, good-breeding is the principal and most necessary one, not only as it is very important in itself; but as it adds great lustre to the more solid advantages both of the heart and the mind.

. . . When an awkward fellow first comes into a room it is highly probable that his sword gets between his legs, and throws him down, or makes him stumble at least; when he has recovered this accident, he goes and places himself in the very place of the whole room where he should not; there he soon lets his hat fall down; and, taking it up again, throws down his cane; in recovering his cane, his hat falls a second time; so that he is a quarter of an hour before he is in order again. If he drinks tea or coffee, he certainly scalds his mouth, and lets either the cup or the saucer fall, and spills the tea or coffee in his breeches. At dinner, his awkwardness distinguishes itself particularly, as he has more to do: there he holds his knife, fork, and spoon differently from other people; eats with his knife to the great danger of his mouth, picks his teeth with his fork, and puts his spoon, which has been in his throat twenty times, into the dishes again. If he is to carve, he can never hit the joint; but, in his vain efforts to cut through the bone, scatters the sauce in everybody's face. He generally daubs himself with soup and grease, though his napkin is commonly stuck through a button-hole, and tickles his chin. When he drinks, he infallibly coughs in his glass, and besprinkles the company. Besides all this, he has strange tricks and gestures; such as snuffing up his nose, making faces, putting his fingers in his nose, or blowing it and looking afterwards in his handkerchief, so as to make the company sick. His hands are troublesome to him, when he has not something in them, and he does not know where to put them; but they are in perpetual motion between his bosom and his breeches: he does not wear his clothes, and in short does nothing, like other people. All this, I own, is not in any degree criminal; but it is highly disagreeable and ridiculous in company, and ought most carefully to be avoided by whoever desires to please.

From this account of what you should not do, you may easily

judge what you should do; and a due attention to the manners of people of fashion, and who have seen the world, will make it habitual and familiar to you.

There is, likewise, an awkwardness of expression and words, most carefully to be avoided; such as false English, bad pronunciation, old sayings, and common proverbs; which are so many proofs of having kept bad and low company. . . .

. . . Adieu! Direct your next to me, *chez* Monsieur Chabert, Banquier, *à* Paris; and take care that I find the improvements I expect at my return.

❖

The Growth of London

While some allowance must be made for literary exaggeration, this account does reflect the changes occurring in London in the mid-eighteenth century.

Source: T. Smollett, *Humphry Clinker* (1872 ed.) p. 118

London is literally new to me; new in its streets, houses, and even in its situation; as the Irishman said, 'London is now gone out of town.' What I left open fields, producing hay and corn, I now find covered with streets and squares, and palaces, and churches. I am credibly informed, that in the space of seven years, eleven thousand new houses have been built in one quarter of Westminster, exclusive of what is daily added to other parts of this unwieldy metropolis. Pimlico and Knightsbridge are now almost joined to Chelsea and Kensington; and if this infatuation continues for half a century, I suppose the whole county of Middlesex will be covered with brick.

It must be allowed, indeed, for the credit of the present age, that London and Westminster are much better paved and lighted than they were formerly. The new streets are spacious, regular, and airy; and the houses generally convenient. The bridge at Blackfriars is a noble monument of taste and public-spirit. I wonder how they stumbled upon a work of such magnificence and utility. But, notwithstanding these improvements, the capital is become an overgrown monster; which, like a dropsical head, will in time leave the body and extremities without nourishment and support. The absurdity will appear in its full force, when we consider that one sixth part of the natives of this whole extensive kingdom is crowded within the bills of mortality. What wonder that our villages are depopulated, and our farms in want of day-labourers? The abolition of small farms is but one cause of the decrease of population. Indeed, the incredible increase of horses and black cattle, to answer the purposes of luxury, requires a prodigious quantity of hay and grass, which are raised and managed without much labour; but a number of hands will always be wanted for the different branches of agriculture, whether the farms be large or small. The tide of luxury has swept all the inhabitants from the open country—the poorest squire, as well as the richest peer, must have his house in town, and make a figure with an extraordinary number of domestics. The plough-boys, cow-herds, and lower hinds are debauched and seduced by the appearance and discourse of those coxcombs in livery, when they make their summer excursions. They desert their dirt and drudgery, and swarm up to London, in hopes of getting into service, where they can live luxuriously and wear fine clothes, without being obliged to work; for idleness is natural to man. Great numbers of these, being disappointed in their expectation, become thieves and sharpers; and London being an immense wilderness, in which there is neither watch nor ward of any signification, nor any order or police, affords them lurking-places as well as prey.

There are many causes that contribute to the daily increase of this enormous mass, but they may be all resolved into the grand source of luxury and corruption. About five and twenty years ago, very few, even of the most opulent citizens of London kept any equipage, or even any servants in livery. Their tables produced nothing but plain boiled and roasted, with a bottle of port and a tankard of beer. At present, every trader in any degree of credit, every broker and attorney, maintains a couple of footmen, a coach-man, and postilion. He has his town-house, and his country-house, his coach, and his post-chaise. His wife and daughters appear in the richest stuffs, bespangled with diamonds. They frequent the court, the opera, the theatre, and the masquerade. They hold assemblies at their own houses; they make sumptuous entertainments, and treat with the richest wines of Bordeaux, Burgundy, and Champagne. The substantial tradesman, who was wont to pass his evenings at the ale-house for fourpence half-penny, now spends three shillings at the tavern, while his wife keeps card-tables at home; she must likewise have fine clothes, her chaise, or pad, with country lodgings, and go three times a week to public diversions. Every clerk, apprentice, and even waiter of tavern or coffeehouse, maintains a gelding by himself, or in partnership, and assumes the air and apparel of a *petit maître*. The gayest places of public entertainment are filled with fashionable figures; which, upon inquiry, will be found to be journeymen tailors, serving-men, and abigails, disguised like their betters.

In short, there is no distinction or subordination left. The different departments of life are jumbled together—the hod-carrier, the low mechanic, the tapster, the publican, the shop-keeper, the pettifogger,[1] the citizen, and courtier, all tread upon the kibes of one another: actuated by the demons of profligacy and licentiousness, they are seen everywhere rambling, riding, rolling, rushing, jostling, mixing, bouncing, cracking, and crashing in one vile ferment of stupidity and corruption. All is tumult and hurry; one would imagine they were impelled by some disorder of the brain, that will not suffer them to be at rest. The foot-passengers run along as if they were pursued by bailiffs. The porters and chairmen trot with their burthens. People, who keep their own equipages, drive through the streets at full speed. Even citizens, physicians, and apothecaries, glide in their chariots like lightning. The hackney-coachmen make their horses smoke, and the pavement shakes under them; and I have actually seen a waggon pass through Piccadilly at the hand-gallop. In a word, the whole nation seems to be running out of their wits. . . .

❖

---

[1] A kind of minor solicitor, dealing with petty cases.

Watering Places

Bath was easily the most popular of the spas; taking the waters there became the fashionable pastime.

Source: T. Smollett, *Humphry Clinker* (1872 ed.) p. 49

... Bath is to me a new world. All is gaiety, good-humour, and diversion. The eye is continually entertained with the splendour of dress and equipage; and the ear with the sound of coaches, chaises, chairs, and other carriages. The merry bells ring round, from morn till night. Then we are welcomed by the city waits in our own lodgings; we have music in the Pump-room every morning, cotillions every forenoon in the rooms, balls twice a week, and concerts every other night, besides private assemblies and parties without number . . . The Square, the Circus, and the Parades, put you in mind of the sumptuous palaces represented in prints and pictures; and the new buildings, such as Princes-row, Harlequin's-row, Bladud's-row, and twenty other rows, look like so many enchanted castles, raised on hanging terraces.

At eight in the morning, we go in dishabille to the Pump-room which is crowded like a Welsh fair, and there you see the highest quality, and the lowest trades folk, jostling each other, without ceremony, hail-fellow well met. The noise of the music playing in the gallery, the heat and flavour of such a crowd, and the hum and buzz of their conversation, gave me the headache and vertigo the first day; but, afterwards, all these things became familiar, and even agreeable. Right under the Pump-room windows is the King's Bath; a huge cistern, where you see the patients up to their necks in hot water. The ladies wear jackets and petticoats of brown linen, with chip hats, in which they fix their handkerchiefs to wipe the sweat from their faces, but, truly, whether it is owing to the steam that surrounds them, or the heat of the water, or the nature of the dress, or to all these causes together, they look so flushed, and so frightful, that I always turn my eyes another way. . . .

The pumper, with his wife and servant, attend within a bar; and the glasses, of different sizes, stand ranged in order before them, so you have nothing to do but to point at that which you choose, and it is filled immediately, hot and sparkling from the pump. It is the only hot water I could ever drink, without being sick. Far from having that effect, it is rather agreeable to the taste, grateful to the stomach and reviving to the spirits. You cannot imagine what wonderful cures it performs. My uncle began with it the other day; but he made wry faces in drinking, and I'm afraid he will leave it off. . . .

Hard by the Pump-room, is a coffee-house for the ladies, but my aunt says, young girls are not admitted, insomuch as the conversation turns upon politics, scandal, philosophy, and other subjects above our capacity; but we are allowed to accompany them to the booksellers' shops, which are charming places of resort; where we read novels, plays, pamphlets, and newspapers, for so small a subscription as a crown a quarter; and in these offices of intelligence (as my brother calls them) all the reports of the day, and all the private transactions of the Bath, are first entered and discussed. From the booksellers' shops, we make a tour through the milliners and toymen; and commonly stop at Mr Gill's the pastry-cook, to take a jelly, a tart, or a small basin of vermicelli.

There is, moreover, another place of entertainment on the other side of the water opposite to the Grove, to which the company cross over in a boat. It is called Spring-gardens; a sweet retreat, laid out in walks and ponds, and parterres of flowers; and there is a long room for breakfasting and dancing. . . .

After all, the great scenes of entertainment at Bath, are the two public rooms; where the company meet alternately every evening. They are spacious, lofty, and, when lighted up, appear very striking. They are generally crowded with well-dressed people, who drink tea in separate parties, play at cards, walk, or sit and chat together, just as they are disposed. Twice a week there is a ball; the expense of which is defrayed by a voluntary subscription among the gentlemen; and every subscriber has three tickets. . .

◆

Popular Pastimes

i. Cock-Fighting

Source: C. de Saussure, *A Foreign View of England in the Reigns of George I and George II* (1902) p. 280

Plate 19

They are large but short-legged birds, their feathers are scarce, they have no crests to speak of, and are very ugly to look at. Some of these fighting-cocks are celebrated, and have pedigrees like gentlemen of good family, some of them being worth five or six guineas. I am told that when transported to France they degenerate—their strength and courage disappear, and they become like ordinary cocks.

The stage on which they fight is round and small. One of the cocks is released, and struts about proudly for a few seconds. He is then caught up and his enemy appears. When the bets are made, one of the cocks is placed on either end of the stage; they are armed with silver spurs, and immediately rush at each other and fight furiously. It is surprising to see the ardour and strength, and courage of these little birds, for they rarely give up till one of them is dead. The spectators are ordinarily composed of common people, and the noise is terrible, and it is impossible to hear yourself speak unless you shout. At Whitehall Cockpit, on the contrary, where the spectators are mostly people of a certain rank, the noise is much less; but would you believe that at this place several hundred pounds are sometimes lost and won? Cocks will sometimes fight a whole hour before one or the other is victorious; at other times one may get killed at once. You sometimes see a cock ready to fall and apparently die, seeming to have no more strength, and suddenly it will regain all its vigour, fight with renewed courage, and kill his enemy. Sometimes a cock will be seen vanquishing his opponent, and thinking he is dead (if cocks can think), jump on the body of the bird and crow lustily with triumph, when the fallen bird will unexpectedly revive and slay the victor. Of course, such cases are very rare, but their possibility makes the fight very exciting.

ii. *Bull-Baiting*

Source: M. Misson, *Memoirs and Observations* (1719) p. 24

Here follows the manner of those bull-baitings which are so much talked of: they tie a rope to the root of the horns of the ox or bull, and fasten the other end of the cord to an iron ring fixed to a stake driven into the ground; so that this cord being about 15 feet long, the bull is confined to a sphere of about 30 foot diameter. Several butchers, or other gentlemen, that are desirous to exercise their dogs, stand round about, each holding his own by the ears, and when the sport begins, they let loose one of the dogs. The dog runs at the bull; the bull immovable looks down upon the dog with an eye of scorn and only turns a horn to him to hinder him from coming near. The dog is not daunted at this; he runs round him and tries to get beneath his belly in order to seize him by the muzzle or the dewlap. The bull then puts himself into a posture of defence. He beats the ground with his feet, which he joins together as close as possible, and his chief aim is not to gore the dog with the point of his horn (when the bull's horns are too sharp they put them into a kind of wooden sheath) but to slide one of them under the dog's belly (who creeps close to the ground to hinder it), and to throw him so high in the air that he may break his neck in the fall. This often happens. When the dog thinks he is sure of fixing his teeth, a turn of the horn, which seems to be done with all the negligence in the world, gives him a sprawl thirty feet high, and puts him in danger of a damnable squelch when he comes down. This danger would be unavoidable if the dog's friends were not ready beneath him, some with their backs to give him a soft reception, and others with long poles, which they offer him slantways so that sliding down them, it may break the force of his fall. Notwithstanding all this care, a toss generally makes him sing to a very scurvy tune and draw his phiz into a pitiful grimace. But unless he is totally stunned with the fall, he is sure to crawl again towards the bull, with his old antipathy, come on't what will. Sometimes a second frisk into the air disables him for ever from playing his old tricks. But sometimes too, he fastens upon his enemy and when once he has seized him with his eye-teeth, he sticks to him like a leech and would sooner die than leave his hold. Then the bull bellows and bounds and kicks about to shake off the dog. By his leaping the dog seems to be no manner of weight to him, though in all appearance he puts him to great pain. In the end, either the dog tears out the piece he has laid hold on, and falls, or else remains fixed to him with an obstinacy that would never end if they did not pull him off. To call him away would be in vain; to give him a hundred blows would be as much so; you might cut him to pieces joint by joint before he would let him loose. What is to be done then? While some hold the bull, others thrust staves into the dog's mouth and open it by main force. This is the only way to part them.

❧

The Sufferings of the Poor

Source: Henry Fielding, *A Proposal for Making an Effectual Provision for the Poor* (1753) p. 9

. . . The sufferings of the poor are, indeed, less observed than their misdeeds; not from any want of compassion, but because they are less known; and this is the true reason why we so often hear them mentioned with abhorrence, and so seldom with pity. But if we were to make a progress through the outskirts of this town, and look into the habitations of the poor, we should there behold such pictures of human misery as must move the compassion of every heart that deserves the name of human. . . .

. . . That such wretchedness as this is so little lamented, arises therefore from its being so little known; but, if this be the case with the sufferings of the poor, it is not so with their misdeeds. They starve, and freeze, and rot among themselves; but they beg, and steal, and rob among their betters. There is not a parish in the

Liberty of Westminster which doth not raise thousands annually for the poor, and there is not a street in that Liberty which doth not swarm all day with beggars, and all night with thieves. Stop your coach at what shop you will, however expeditious the tradesman is to attend you, a beggar is commonly beforehand with him; and if you should not directly face his door the tradesman must often turn his head while you are talking to him, or the same beggar, or some other thief at hand, will pay a visit to his shop! I omit to speak of the more open and violent insults which are every day committed on His Majesty's subjects in the streets and highways. They are enough known and enough spoken of. The depredations on property are less noticed, particularly those in the parishes within ten miles of London. To these every man is not obnoxious, and therefore it is not every man's business to suppress them. These are, however, grown to the most deplorable height; insomuch that the gentleman is daily, or rather nightly, plundered of his pleasure, and the farmer of his livelihood.

❖

Infant Mortality

Source: Jonas Hanway, *An Earnest Appeal for Mercy to the Children of the Poor* (1766) p. 4

... One may with great truth assert that many children born of poor, idle, or unfortunate parents, though they should have the best constitutions, yet die in great numbers under 5 years old. ... Many children instead of being nourished with care, by the fostering hand of a wholesome country nurse, are thrust into the impure air of a work-house, into the hands of some careless, worthless young female or decrepit old woman, and inevitably lost for want of such means as the God of Nature, their father as well as ours, has appointed for their preservation.

It is hard to say how many lives these cities have lost, or how many they yet lose annually, by the poverty, filth and vice of parents, which no public institutions in this land of freedom can save; and though we live on as fine a spot as any of the three kingdoms can boast of, yet by being closely built, and many living in confined places, and many too much congregated, joined to the sulphurous air created by so vast a number of coal fires, we must not be surprised that so great a proportion as 20,232 in 43,101, or near 47 per cent, die under 2 years of age: this appears now by an account before me of 1756, 1757, and 1758. The calamities of human life, and the customs of mankind, keep a pretty equal pace, and accordingly we find that—

There were christened in 1764	.. .. ..	16,374
Died under 2 years of age which is 49¼ per cent	..	8,073
Remains	.. ..	8,301

Died more between 2 and 5 years old—1875—which on 16,374 is 11½ per cent and on 8301 is 22½ per cent.

... Never shall I forget the evidence given at Guild-Hall, upon occasion of a master of a workhouse of a large parish, who was challenged for forcing a child from the breast of the mother, and sending it to the Foundling Hospital. He alleged this in his defence: 'We send all our children to the Foundling Hospital: we have not saved one alive for fourteen years. We have no place fit to preserve them in; the air is too confined ...' Of the same nature was another parish, some years before the Foundling Hospital was opened, wherein it appeared, that of 54 children born, and taken into their workhouse, not one outlived the year in which it was born or taken in. This seemed to be so incredible, that I went to the workhouse to inquire into the fact, and found it true. ...

... Mrs Poole [a nurse] had, in the year of our Lord MDCCLXV, the nursing of 23 children belonging to St Clement Danes ... The account of the 23 children stands thus:

Discharged at the age of 2 years	1
„ „ „ „ 5 months	1
Remaining alive	3
Departed out of this transitory life, in her hands, after breathing the vital air about one month	18

For this piece of service to the Parish, Mrs Poole has been paid 2s each per week, which, considering the importance of the enterprise, must be deemed a very moderate price.

❖

Prisons

i. *Source: State Trials* xvii. pp. 300–2

The Committee of enquiry found amongst other things, That the said Thomas Bambridge . . . caused one Jacob Mendez Solas[1] . . . to be seized, fettered, and carried to Corbett's, the spunging-house, and there kept for upwards of a week, and when brought back into the prison, Bambridge caused him to be turned into the dungeon, called the Strong Room of the Master's side.

This place is a vault like those in which the dead are interred, and wherein the bodies of persons dying in the said prison are usually deposited, till the coroner's inquest hath passed upon them; it has no chimney nor fire-place, nor any light but what comes over the door, or through a hole of about eight inches square. It is neither paved nor boarded; and the rough bricks appear both on the sides and top, being neither wainscotted nor plastered: what adds to the dampness and stench of the place is, its being built over the common sewer . . . In this miserable place the poor wretch was kept by the said Bambridge, manacled and shackled, for near two months. At length, on receiving five guineas from Mr Kemp, a friend of Solas's, Bambridge released the prisoner from his cruel confinement. But though his chains were taken off, his terror still remained, and the unhappy man was prevailed upon by that terror, not only to labour gratis, for the said Bambridge, but to swear also at random all that he hath required of him; and the Committee themselves saw an instance of the deep impression his sufferings had made upon him; for on his surmising, from something said,

[1] A Portuguese debtor.

that Bambridge was to return again, as Warden of the Fleet, he fainted, and the blood started out of his mouth and nose. . . .

Next morning the said Bambridge entered the prison with a detachment of soldiers, and ordered the prisoner [another debtor] to be dragged to the lodge, and ironed with great irons, on which he desired to know for what cause, and by what authority he was to be so cruelly used? Bambridge replied, 'It was by his own authority, and damn him he would do it, and have his life.' The prisoner desired that he might be carried before a magistrate, that he might know his crime before he was punished; but Bambridge refused, and put irons upon his legs which were too little, so that in forcing them on, his legs were like to have been broken; and the torture was impossible to be endured. Upon which the prisoner complaining of the grievous pain and the straitness of the irons, Bambridge answered, 'That he did it on purpose to torture him'; on which the prisoner replying 'That by the law of England no man ought to be tortured'; Bambridge declared, 'That he would do it first and answer for it afterwards'; and caused him to be dragged away to the dungeon, where he lay without a bed, loaded with irons so close-rivetted that they kept him in continued torture, and mortified his legs. After long application[1] his irons were changed, and a surgeon directed to dress his legs, but his lameness is not, nor ever can be cured. He was kept in this miserable condition for three weeks, by which his sight is greatly prejudiced, and in danger of being lost.

ii. While the appalling conditions in prisons were generally accepted, reforming minds were already at work, led by John Howard, who anticipated many aspects of modern prison reform.

Source: John Howard, *The State of the Prisons* (1777) p. 40

. . . The first thing to be taken into consideration is the prison itself. Many county gaols and other prisons are so decayed and ruinous or, for other reasons, so totally unfit for the purpose, that new ones must be built in their stead. . . .

. . . I said a gaol should be near a stream; but I must annex this caution, that it be not so near as that either the house or yard

---

[1] i.e. after he had made many applications.

shall be within the reach of floods. This circumstance was so little thought of at Appleby in Westmorland, when their new gaol was first building, that I saw the walls marked from nine inches to three feet high by floods. . . .

. . . That part of the building which is detached from the walls, and contains the men-felons' ward, may be square, or rectangular, raised on arcades, that it may be more airy, and leave under it a dry walk in wet weather. These wards over arcades are also best for safety, for I have found that escapes have been most commonly effected by undermining cells and dungeons. When I went into Horsham gaol with the keeper, we saw a heap of stones and rubbish. The felons had been for two or three days undermining the foundation of their room; and a general escape was intended that night. We were but just in time to prevent it; for it was almost night when we went in. Our lives were at their mercy: but (thank God) they did not attempt to murder us, and rush out. . . .

. . . I wish to have so many small rooms or cabins that each criminal may sleep alone. These rooms to be ten feet high to the crown of the arch, and have double doors, one of them iron-latticed, for the circulation of air. If it be difficult to prevent their being together in the daytime, they should by all means be separated at night. Solitude and silence are favourable to reflection, and may possibly lead them to repentance. Privacy and hours of thoughtfulness are necessary for those who must soon leave the world (yet how contrary to this is our practice! Keepers have assured me, that they have made £5 a day after the condemnation of their prisoners). . . .

. . . The women-felons should be quite separate from the men; and the young criminals from old and hardened offenders. Each of these three classes should also have their day-room or kitchen with a fireplace; and their court and offices all separate. . . .

. . . Debtors and felons should have wards totally separate: the peace, the cleanliness, the health and morals of debtors cannot be secured otherwise. . . .

. . . Constant separation is desirable. The gaol will by that means be kept cleaner; and if the smallpox, or the gaol-fever, should infect one ward, the other at a distance may be free from it. This would also remove the objection that is now made against permitting debtors to work: that is, the danger of their furnishing felons with tools for mischief, or escape.

In the debtors' ward there should be a day-room or kitchen; also a large workshop for such as are willing to work. Some few gaols have the latter; and in them I have seen basket-makers, shoemakers, etc., employed in their several trades; preserving their habit of industry; contributing to the support of their families, and lightening the burthen that by their imprisonment falls on the respective parishes. Here I would observe, that wherever the windows are glazed there should be casements; for I have found the debtors' rooms, and passages of many town and city gaols very offensive for want of apertures.

Index

Italic figures refer to plate numbers